Backyard Building

Backyard Building

JEANIE & DAVID STILES

Treehouses, Sheds, Arbors, Gates and Other Garden Projects

Designs and Illustrations by David Stiles

COUNTRYMAN KNOW HOW

Illustrations © David Stiles

Photo Credits:
    All photos are by Jeanie Stiles unless otherwise noted below:
    Simon Jutras: Cover, Page 218, 240
    R.J.T. Haynes: Page 8 and back cover (Authors' photo), pages 41, 72, 74, 75, 80, 217 (lower left), 220, 222, 223, 226, 227, 228, 229, 239 (top left), 250 (lower left & right), 251 (left)
    Skip Hine: Page 10, page 46, 47, 59, 62, 82, 86,
    David Stiles: Page 137, 145
    Jon Mulder : Page 151
    Randee Daddona: Page 157 (top), 216 (left)
    Jaime Stiles: Page 162, 163, 164, 165, 167, 216 (right)
    Sara Webb: Page 225

Designed and composed by Nick Caruso

Published by
THE COUNTRYMAN PRESS
P.O. Box 748, Woodstock, VT 05091

Distributed by
W. W. NORTON & COMPANY, INC
500 Fifth Avenue, New York, NY 10110

Printed in the United States

Backyard Building
ISBN 978-1-58157-238-4

10 9 8 7 6 5 4 3 2 1

To Jean and William

To Our Readers

Since many of our readers invariably change our plans to fit their own particular needs, we assume that they will seek qualified, licensed architects or engineers to make more detailed plans for submission to their local building departments as required.

Note: Every effort has been made to design all the projects in this book to be safe and easy to build: however, it is impossible to predict every situation and the ability of each carpenter who builds our projects. Therefore, it is advised that the reader seek advice from a competent on-site expert. Please send us photos of your completed projects—we always love to see them.

Disclaimer: David and Jeanie make no express or implied warranties, including warranties of performance, merchantability, and fitness for a particular purpose regarding this information. Your use of this information is at your own risk. You assume full responsibility and risk of loss resulting form the use of this information. The authors and publisher will not be responsible for any direct, special, indirect, incidental, consequential or punitive damages or any other damage whatsoever.

Contents

Introduction

If you mention "backyard building" to most people, they will immediately think of some practical, if not downright utilitarian structure such as a toolshed, workshop or small office: in a busy modern world, it seems, even the garden has to work for a living. But a backyard—a garden, your very own bit of the great outdoors—is also for enjoyment, relaxation and entertainment, and there are designs here for playhouses, treehouses, pergolas, summerhouses, and outdoor seating, which could be the focal point of an existing beautiful garden or the incentive to get out there and finally tackle those weeds.

We still hope that in these pages you will find the perfect shed, if that's what you're looking for—either straight from our plans or by using them as a springboard for your own ideas and adaptations, as this book is intended to be as much inspiration as simple "how to." Some projects are described in greater detail, others in more general terms—as, once you understand the principles of construction (which are not as daunting as they might at first appear), you can see how to make more or less anything. We've included designs that could be built by almost anyone in a few hours, as well as more ambitious and elaborate ones requiring a bit more experience and dedication; but all of them are within the capabilities of the average handyman with average tools. If you've never done carpentry before—or not since being forced to in school—try one of the easier projects first: you may be surprised at how quickly you discover your inner craftsman or craftswoman. Enjoy your backyard building.

Everything is easier when you know how—and here's an assortment of useful information and tips we've learned along the way, to help the job go smoothly.

Wood

Today's pressure-treated (P.T.) wood is non-toxic ACQ, but we still recommend washing your hands after using it. (Don't use the scraps in your fireplace either.) If using it for posts that are to be buried in the ground, make sure the label says "for ground contact." Most of the pressure-treated wood sold in the US is made from southern pine, which is actually a very pretty type of wood - harder, stronger, and cheaper than white pine. If possible, pick out the lumber yourself, since quality inevitably varies. You should apply clear preservative to cut surfaces, even on pressure-treated wood.

TRANSPORTING LUMBER

If your car has roof bars, you can save a lot of money on delivery charges for lumber—even bulky items such as plywood sheets. Take two 2×4s 48" long, cut notches in the bottoms to fit over the roof bars, and secure them with duct tape or strapping tape. (Use stainless-steel wire if you are going long distances.)

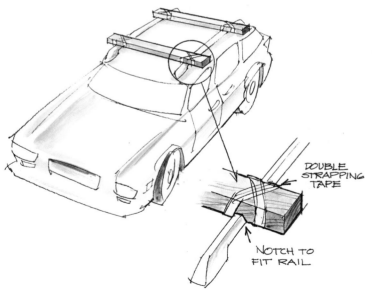

DOUBLE STRAPPING TAPE

NOTCH TO FIT RAIL

Fasteners

SCREWS

Screws come in several types, from your grandfather's slotted-head screw to the old standard Phillips head, the newer square head and the most recent improvement, the star head. Unless you want to drive yourself crazy, decide on one type of screw and stick to it—it's annoying to pick up your screwdriver and find that the bit doesn't match the head of the screw in your other hand. Star-drive screws are the easiest to use because they are least likely to slip, but they're also the most expensive.

SLOT   PHILLIPS   SQUARE   STAR

NAILS

Although cheaper than screws, nails are more difficult to remove if you make a mistake - and it can be hard to keep the workpiece in position while hammering a nail in. They don't work well in end-grain wood, but are useful where the load is perpendicular to the nail and to the grain (as in shingling or sheathing). For outdoor applications, only galvanized or rustproof nails should be used.

BOLTS

Bolts are the strongest fasteners of all, and will join two pieces of wood with a vise-like grip. They have the added advantage of being easily removed; however, they have to be carefully measured, and in some situations (such as treehouses and playhouses) must be counterbored so that the sharp ends don't become a hazard. The counterbored hole has to be large enough for a socket wrench to tighten the nut.

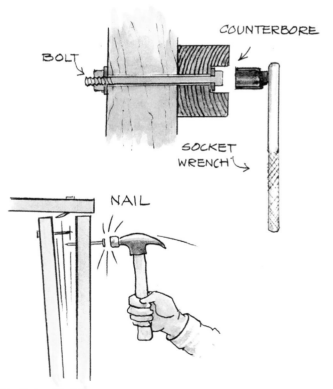

LAG SCREWS

We use lag screws far more than bolts, because you don't have to be too exact about measuring them and there's no nut & washer needed on the other end. They are ideal for attaching a beam to a tree; but make sure the screw threads catch into the fibers of the tree: drill a pilot hole slightly narrower than the lag screw, and hammer the head of the screw after each turn of the wrench until you feel the threads really biting into the tree. If it turns too easily, you will know it's stripping the wood and not really holding.

PILOT HOLES

A pilot hole makes the screw go in more easily and accurately, and helps to prevent the wood splitting. The pilot hole in the first piece of wood should be the same diameter as the shank of the screw; in the second it should be narrower, to let the screw threads 'bite'.

When building play equipment for children, recess the sharp heads of bolts or screws by drilling a counterbore hole as wide as the washer before drilling the main hole; otherwise the spade bit has nothing to hold onto and will tear the wood.

TOENAILING

Begin by placing the stud ¼" short of the intended position. Start the nail at an angle and begin hammering in: the last few strokes will knock the stud into place.

Use 16d 3½" nails

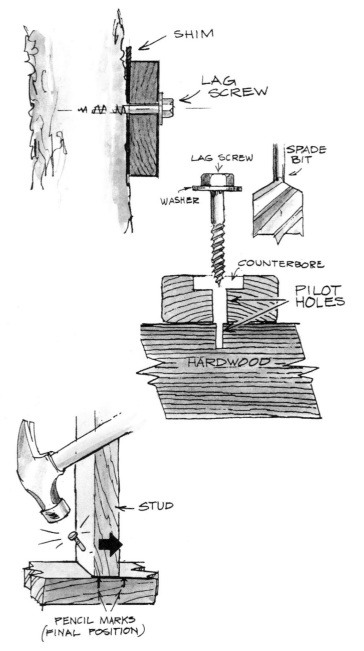

SHIM

LAG SCREW

LAG SCREW

WASHER

SPADE BIT

COUNTERBORE

PILOT HOLES

HARDWOOD

STUD

PENCIL MARKS (FINAL POSITION)

Sanding Block

One of the best and most-used tools in our shop is a sanding block. We make our own by gluing sandpaper to both sides of a scrap piece of 1×4; if the kids are helping with your projects, make a narrower block (1×3) to fit their smaller hands. The wooden block is essential for sanding a flat surface. We use several blocks with various grades (grits) of sandpaper from 120 (fine) to 40 (coarse). Attach the sandpaper to the block using regular carpenter's glue, and clamp it between two boards to dry. When cutting the sandpaper to fit the block, allow ⅛" of overhang—this allows you to sand hard-to-reach corners, cracks, and so on.

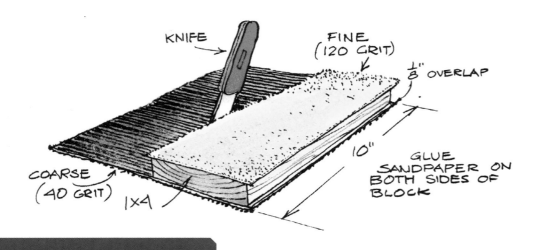

KNIFE

FINE (120 GRIT)

⅛" OVERLAP

COARSE (40 GRIT)

1×4

10"

GLUE SANDPAPER ON BOTH SIDES OF BLOCK

SANDING TIP

Sand in the direction of the grain and work from coarse to fine. You can buy a "bargain box" of assorted, industrial sandpaper remnants at www.woodworkingosp.com.

Easy-to-Make Windows

You can order a single-sash or barn window from your lumberyard, but it's easy to make your own if you have a table saw. It requires only one piece of glass (or plastic): muntin bars on both sides of the pane give the impression of truly divided lites (see page 108). You can also make a log window if you choose (see page 166).

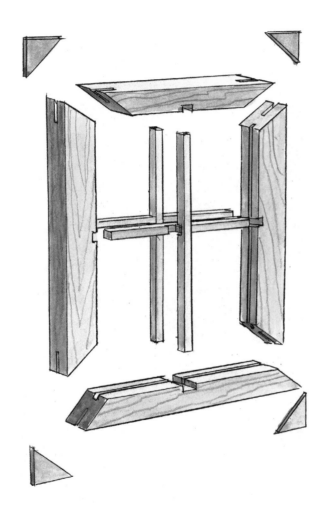

17

Basic Backyard Projects

1

Gates and seats need to be functional, but they can be attractive too—we show you how. Some of these designs serve more practical purposes than others, but all are intended to enhance their setting and increase your enjoyment of your own backyard.

Deck with Benches

Find a secluded spot in your backyard or garden, and build this small deck as a retreat—a place to read, relax and meditate. A deck for these purposes need not be big—8'×8' square is a practical size. Surround it on three sides with rambling Rugosa roses, which will offer their benefits year-round: scent and blooms throughout the summer, rosehips in the fall, and little if no maintenance. Rot-resistant cedar or redwood will weather to a soft gray, blending with the surrounding woods and plantings; or perhaps for that unused damp area, choose pressure-treated wood and set the deck among irises, grasses, cattails and other moisture-loving plants. The design includes a U-shaped bench, just the right size to accommodate a 5'-diameter table and an 8' umbrella. The two rear corners of the bench allow ample space for large pots planted with shrubs or flowers.

MATERIALS

4	8'	2×8 #2 cedar *for deck frame*
2	4'	4×4 #2 cedar *for deck frame posts*
8	5'	4×4 #2 cedar *for seating posts*
3	1'	4×4 #2 cedar *for step posts*
4	8'	2×6 pressure-treated lumber *for deck joists*
2	8'	2×4 pressure-treated lumber *for deck ledges*
1	4'	2×4 pressure-treated lumber *for step support blocks*
1	12'	2×6 pressure-treated lumber *for front step*

26	8'	2×4 #2 cedar *for decking and steps*
5	8'	2×4 #2 cedar *for seat frames*
1	5'	2×4 #2 cedar *for seat front*
12	5'	2×4 #2 cedar *for seat decking*
2	18'	2×4 #2 cedar *for seat ends*
2	10'	2×4 #2 cedar *for triangular seats*
6	5'	2×4 #2 cedar *for seat supports and deck cleats*
2 lbs.		3" galvanized screws *for deck*

Deck

Since the deck will be built on posts, it is not necessary to make the site perfectly level. Begin by screwing two 96"-long 2×8s to two 93"-long 2×8s to form an 8'-square frame. (The front & rear pieces overlap the side pieces.) Check for square by measuring the diagonals, which should be 135¾" from the outsides. Mark the soil directly below each corner, and dig four 30"-deep holes. Cut the 4×4 posts so their tops will be 1½" below the top edge of the deck frame, and place them in the holes. Screw the deck frame to the posts; check levels and backfill, tamping the soil down firmly. Dig two more holes and install additional posts for the front and rear deck frame pieces.

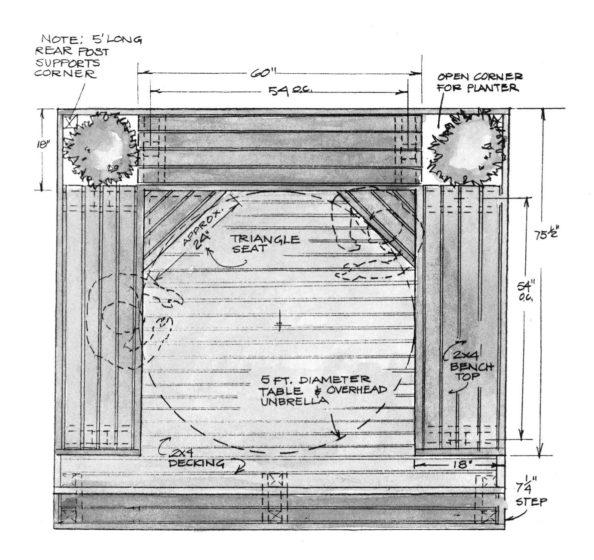

NOTE: 5'LONG REAR POST SUPPORTS CORNER

OPEN CORNER FOR PLANTER

60"

54 o.c.

18"

75½"

54" o.c.

APPROX. 24"

TRIANGLE SEAT

5 FT. DIAMETER TABLE & OVERHEAD UMBRELLA

2×4 BENCH TOP

2×4 DECKING

18"

7¼" STEP

PLAN VIEW
DECK & BENCH

Locating the Seating Posts

On the front and back pieces of the frame, measure in 7¼" from the corners and make a mark. Tie strings to temporary nails placed at these points, and draw the strings across the deck frame from side to side. On the side pieces of the frame, measure 18" from the front and rear corners, mark and attach strings. Dig post holes where the strings intersect, allowing 15½" of post to extend above the frame and strings. Check that all the seating posts are at the same height and in alignment, and backfill the holes.

Floor Joists

Attach four 2×6 floor joists to the 2×8 front and rear deck frame, 1½" below the top so that the 2×4 decking will finish flush with the frame. Attach an 86"-long 2×4 ledge to each side of the frame at the same height, to support the ends of the deck boards.

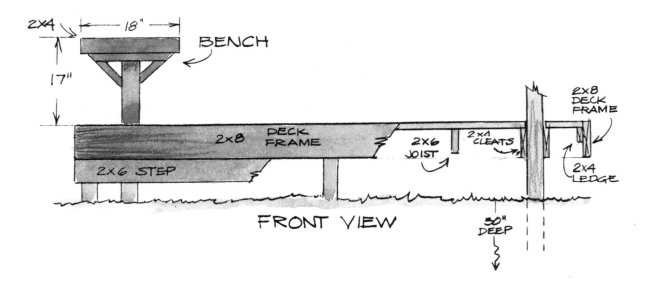

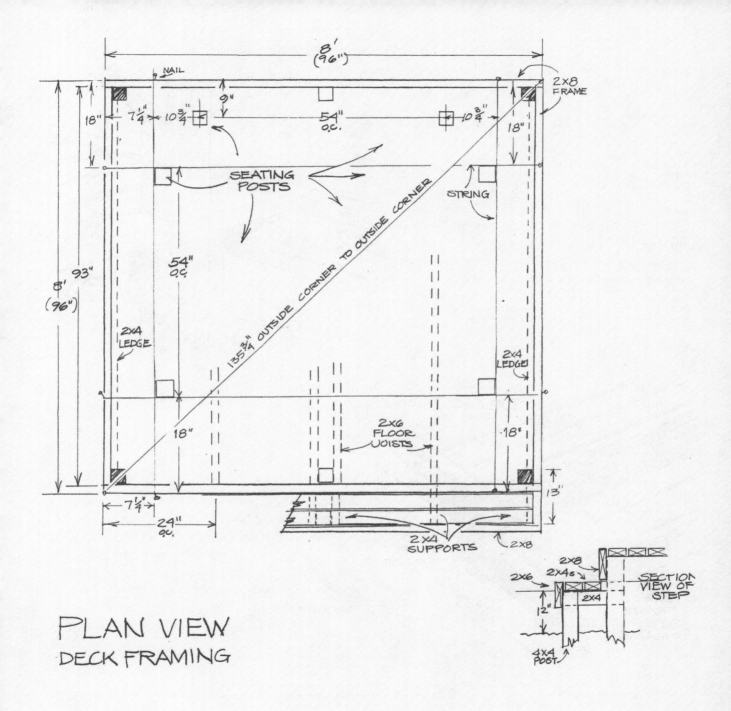

PLAN VIEW
DECK FRAMING

Decking

Install the 2×4 decking, using 16d galvanized nails or 3" galvanized deck screws. Screw short 2×4 cleats to the seating posts, to support the decking where it meets the posts. Allow ¼" spacing between deck boards—or about the thickness of a pencil.

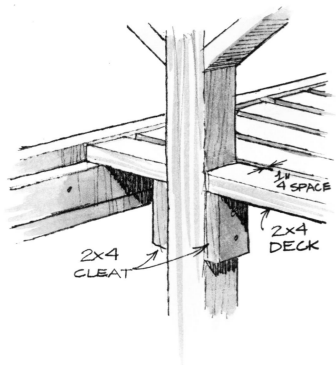

2×4 CLEAT

¼" SPACE

2×4 DECK

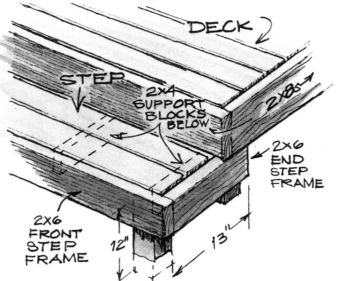

DECK

STEP

2×4 SUPPORT BLOCKS BELOW

2×8s

2×6 END STEP FRAME

2×6 FRONT STEP FRAME

12"

13"L

Step

Frame the step by screwing a 13" length 2×6 to each side corner post. Attach a short 4×4 post to support the open end of each step frame. Nail an 8'-long 2×6 across the front of the step. Add another 4×4 post and 2×6 in the middle, and space six 2×4 support blocks equidistantly apart. Nail the two deck boards to the support blocks.

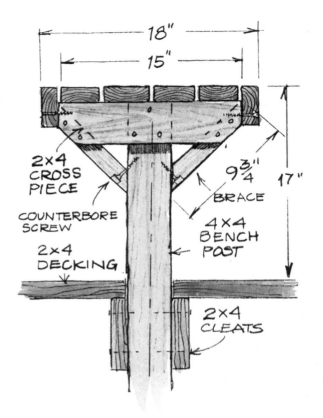

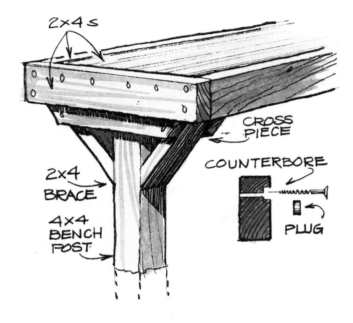

Benches

1. The benches are built out of clear cedar or redwood, supported by V-shaped braces and crosspieces. Cut 12 pieces of 2×4 15" long for the crosspieces, and 12 pieces 9¾" long for the braces. Bevel the ends of the braces at 45 degrees. Screw the crosspieces to the outside and inside of each bench post. Fit the braces to the crosspieces using 3½" galvanized deck screws. Counterbore and screw the bottoms of the braces to the bench posts.

2. Drill ½"-diameter counterbore holes in the 72"-long 2×4 bench framing boards, and screw them to the front and back of the seats. Add 18"-long 2×4 end boards, and plug the counterbored holes with ½" plugs cut from a piece of the same lumber. Attach the remaining four 2×4 seating boards, leaving ¼" between boards.

3. Build the triangular seats by attaching 15"-long 2×4 ledge pieces to the inside corners of the three benches, and screwing 2×4s, mitered at 45 degrees, to the ledges. Make a front edge frame for the seats by mitering both ends of a 2×4. These seats add rigidity to the main benches, and also define the spaces for potted plants.

Covered Garden Seat

Patterns of light filter through the lattice of this relaxing garden seat. Constructed of clear cedar, it is a design both elegant and practical. It could be the focus of a summer garden—covered with tendrils of evening-blooming vines and English ivy—or a seat for two on a porch or patio.

MATERIALS

2	12'	4×4 clear cedar posts *for corner posts*
1	8'	4×4 clear cedar *for horizontal side pieces*
2	8'	4×4 clear cedar *for crosspieces*
8	12'	1×4 clear cedar V-groove *for lower sides & back*
6	10'	1×2 clear cedar *for slats & cleats*
1		4'×8' panel diagonal cedar lattice *for sides & back*
2	6'	2×4 cedar *for rafters*
3	8'	2×2 cedar *for purlins, cross-tie & ridgepole*
3	8'	⁵⁄₄×4 clear cedar *for seat*
1	10'	2×6 clear cedar *for cove molding*
2	8'	1×4 clear cedar *for fascia*
1	3'	¾"-diameter dowel *for plugs*
18		⅜"×6" lag screws
2 lbs.		2" galvanized finishing nails

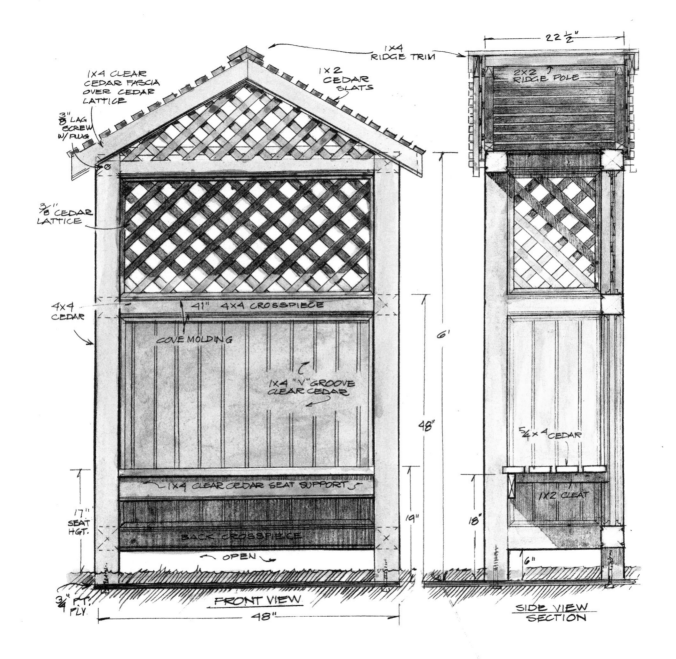

1X4 CLEAR
CEDAR FASCIA
OVER CEDAR
LATTICE

1X4
RIDGE TRIM

1X2
CEDAR
SLATS

22 ½"

2X2
RIDGE POLE

⅜" LAG
SCREW
W/ PLUG

3/8" CEDAR
LATTICE

3/8" CEDAR
LATTICE

4X4
CEDAR

41" 4X4 CROSSPIECE

COVE MOLDING

6'

1X4 "V" GROOVE
CLEAR CEDAR

48"

5/4 X 4 CEDAR

1X4 CLEAR CEDAR SEAT SUPPORT

17"
SEAT
HGT.

19"

1X2 CLEAT

BACK CROSSPIECE

18"

OPEN

6"

¾" FT.
PLY.

FRONT VIEW
48"

SIDE VIEW
SECTION

Wall Frame

Cut the two 4×4 cedar posts to four 6' lengths, and sand smooth using progressively finer grades of 60- to 120-grit sandpaper. Number the top of each post, and draw an arrow showing its relation to the center of the structure, as it's easy to mix up the pieces during assembly. Using a carpenter's square, mark the position of the topmost lag screws, on adjacent faces, 1½" and 2" from one end of each post. Note that the holes are staggered to keep the screws from colliding. Drill ¾"-diameter holes ¾" deep, followed by ⁷⁄₁₆" pilot holes right through the post.

Cut six horizontal side pieces out of 4×4 cedar, 15½" long. Cut four crosspieces out of 4×4 cedar, 41" long. Sand as above.

CENTER

4×4 POSTS
MARKED ON ENDS

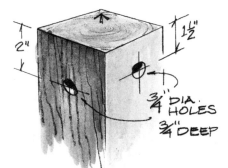

2"

1½"

¾" DIA. HOLES
¾" DEEP

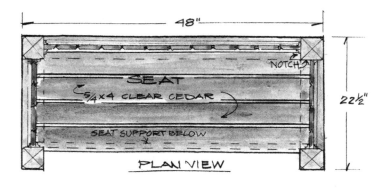

48"

22½"

NOTCH

SEAT
5/4×4 CLEAR CEDAR

SEAT SUPPORT BELOW

PLAN VIEW

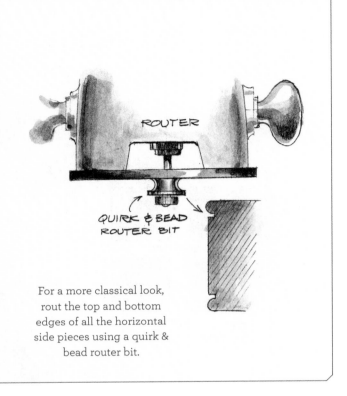

ROUTER

QUIRK & BEAD
ROUTER BIT

For a more classical look, rout the top and bottom edges of all the horizontal side pieces using a quirk & bead router bit.

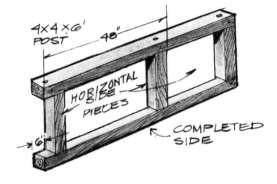

4×4×6' POST

48"

HORIZONTAL SIDE PIECES

6'

COMPLETED SIDE

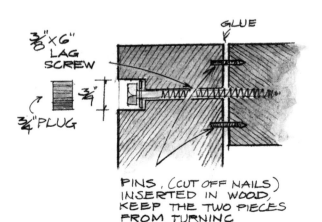

GLUE

3/8"×6" LAG SCREW

3/4"

3/4" PLUG

PINS, (CUT OFF NAILS) INSERTED IN WOOD, KEEP THE TWO PIECES FROM TURNING

To assemble the sides, stand three horizontal side pieces on end, position a post on top of them, and glue and screw each joint with a ⅜"×6" counterbored lag screw using a socket wrench. Turn the assembly over and attach the second post.

To prevent the horizontal side pieces from turning once installed, hammer 2" nails halfway into the side of each vertical post, and cut off the heads with a bolt cutter. When you screw the post down, these points will press into the soft end grain of the horizontal beams and lock them in place.

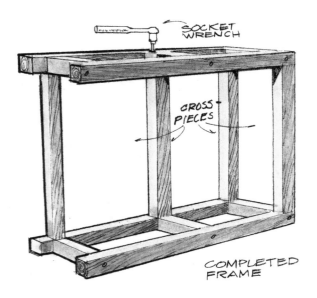

SOCKET WRENCH

CROSS PIECES

COMPLETED FRAME

Lattice and Siding

Measure the uppermost openings in the sides and back of the covered seat. Using an electric jigsaw, cut the lattice to fit inside the openings. Install the lattice, using ¾" cove molding nailed to both sides.

Install the 1×4 V-groove vertical boards in the lower side and back openings, using ¾"×¾" cove molding to secure them to the horizontal 4×4s.

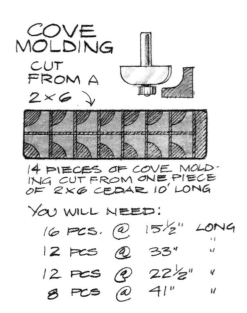

COVE MOLDING CUT FROM A 2×6 ↓

14 PIECES OF COVE MOLD- ING CUT FROM ONE PIECE OF 2×6 CEDAR 10' LONG

YOU WILL NEED:

16 PCS. @ 15½" LONG

12 PCS @ 33" "

12 PCS @ 22½" "

8 PCS @ 41" "

Lay one of the assembled sides flat on the ground, and stand the four crosspieces on it, aligning them with the horizontal side pieces. Apply epoxy glue to the exposed ends. With an assistant, carefully position the second side over the ends of the cross-pieces. Use three bar clamps to hold the assembly in place, and screw ⅜"×6" lag screws through the side into the ends of the crosspieces. Turn the assembly over and follow the same procedure for the second side. Stand up the structure. For a finished look, plug the holes and sand them smooth.

Roof Frames

To make the roof rafters, cut four pieces of 2×4, 32¼" long. Cut the ends of each piece at a 30-degree angle. Measure 1½" up from the bottom end of each piece, and cut a right-angle notch (bird's mouth), 1⅛"×1⅛".

For the purlins, cut three pieces of 2×2 cedar 22½" long. Cut a 1½"×1½" notch in the rafters to accept the 2×2 purlins, 1¼" from the bottom ends. Cut a 1½" notch out of the peak, where the rafters meet, to support the 2×2 ridgepole. Glue and screw the pieces together, using temporary blocks to keep the rafters from spreading. Make sure the pieces are square with one another and that the inside measurement between the bird's mouth cuts is 48".

When the glue has dried, cut two 2×2 cross-ties 44" long, and cut the ends at 30 degrees. Glue and screw the cross-ties to the bottoms of the rafters. Set the assembled roof frame on the main frame, and secure by screwing down through the cross-ties into the top of the posts.

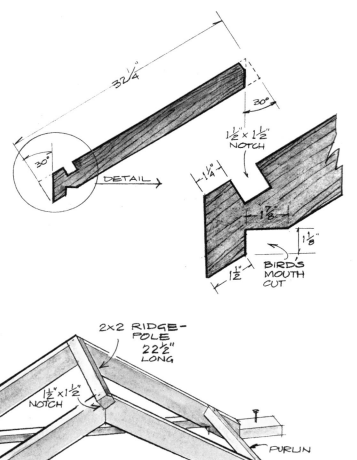

Roof Trim

Cut, glue and nail diagonal cedar lattice to the front and back gables of the roof frame, allowing each piece to overlap the top of the main frame by 1⅛". Cut the top of the lattice flush with the tops of the rafters. Trim the front and sides of the roof with clear 1×4 cedar, using 2" galvanized finishing nails. Begin with the side trim, nailing it to the ends of the rafters; then cut the front trim pieces to meet at the peak, each at a 39-degree angle. Trial-fit them together. Hold the front trim pieces in place and mark on the back where they meet the side pieces. Cut where marked and nail in place, using 2" galvanized nails spaced 8"–9" apart.

Cover the roof with 1×2 cedar slats 27½" long, spaced 1" apart and overlapping the front and back fascia trim boards by 1".

Seat

Measure the inside width from side panel to side panel (about 43"), and cut six pieces of ⁵⁄₄×4 clear cedar for the seat. Screw one piece to the inside backs of the two front posts, 18" up from the bottom of the posts, to provide a lateral support for the seat. Nail a 1×2 support cleat across each side, 18" up from the bottom. Install the remaining ⁵⁄₄×4 cedar boards for the seat, using 2" finishing nails nailed to the cleats and the lateral support. The front and back seat boards will have to be notched around the vertical corner posts.

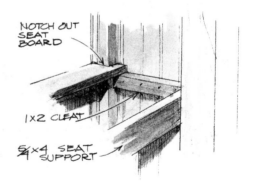

NOTCH OUT SEAT BOARD

1×2 CLEAT

⁵⁄₄×4 SEAT SUPPORT

1×4 RIDGE TRIM

1×2 ROOF SLATS

1×4 FASCIA TRIM

1⅛" OVERLAP

LATTICE

NOTE

For an elegant touch, chamfer the outside edges of the corner posts, using a 45-degree bevel router bit.

Picnic Table

After working in the city all winter, we celebrate summer by spending as much time as possible outdoors: working, relaxing and, of course, dining "al fresco." Most of our meals are eaten at the long picnic table that we built under a dogwood tree. When night falls, we light hurricane lanterns, build a wood fire and cook out as often as possible. Friends and relatives join us on weekends, gathering together at what has become an indispensable landmark representing years of pleasant meals and memories. When the first chill sets in, we bundle up; and only when it becomes teeth-chatteringly cold do we reluctantly head indoors to eat.

MATERIALS

1	10'	6×6 pressure-treated lumber *for posts*
1	6'	2×8 pressure-treated lumber *for table supports*
10	8'	2×4 redwood *for table top*
2		80lb. bags concrete mix *for base collar*

1 lb. 3" galvanized deck screws

1 box ½" wood plugs *for table top*

1 quart water sealer or stain

Posts

Cut the two 59"-long posts out of 6×6 lumber. Using a post hole digger, dig two holes approximately 32" deep and 54" apart; place a brick or stone at the bottom for the posts to rest on. Lay a 2×4 across the two supports and check for level. They should be 27½" high (assuming level ground), plumb, and in line with each other. Backfill the holes, tamping and compressing the soil as you fill. Continue checking with a level to make sure the posts don't stray out of alignment. Don't fill the hole completely with dirt: the top portion should be concreted. Measure out 4" around each post and dig a 3"-deep circular trench (about 14" diameter) where it meets the ground, and fill this with a stiff concrete mix. Mound up the concrete with a trowel, so rainwater will be shed from the surface. Let the concrete set overnight.

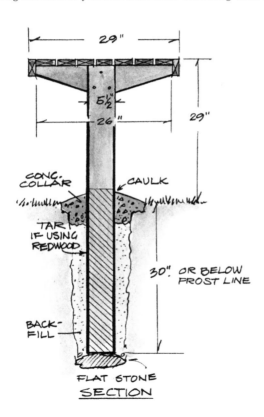

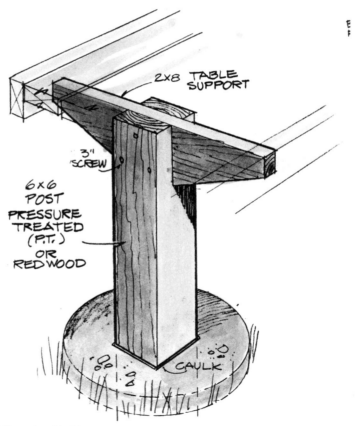

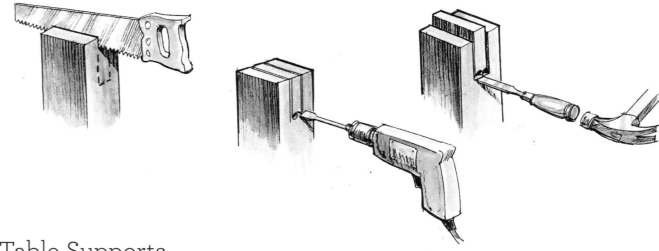

Table Supports

The posts and table supports form a "T" on which the table top rests. Cut the two 26"-long table supports out of 2×8s, and shape the ends as shown (see detail).

Mark a 1½"-wide slot 7¼" deep in the center top of each post, at right angles to the length of the table. Make the vertical cuts with a ripsaw. Drill a ½" hole through the bottom of the cut, and clear out the inside of each slot with a ½" chisel. Center the supports in the slots and drive three 2" galvanized deck screws through each side of the legs into the table supports.

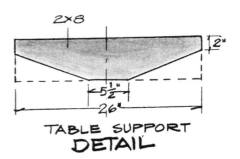

TABLE SUPPORT
DETAIL

Table Top

Cut seven pieces of redwood 2×4, 93" long. Lay the 2×4s across the table supports, spaced ¼" apart and aligned evenly at the ends. Draw a line across the 2×4s above the center of each table support, and drill a ½"-diameter counterbored hole ½" deep in the center of each 2×4. Screw all seven pieces to the table support (see plan view).

For the table edging, cut two pieces 29" long and two pieces 8' long. Trim the ends at a 45-degree angle. Drill ½"-diameter counterbored holes at intervals, ¾" down from the top edge, and screw the edging to the tabletop.

Finishing

Fill the screw holes with ½" plugs. It looks better (and is easy) to make your own plugs from a scrap piece of matching redwood, using a special bit called a "plug cutter" if you have a drill press; otherwise, use birch or cherrywood plugs. Glue, and gently tap the plugs in with a wooden mallet. Use medium (80-grit) sandpaper to smooth the plugs and the table surface.

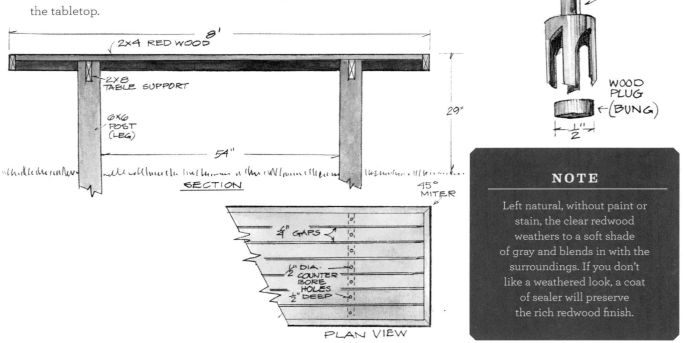

NOTE

Left natural, without paint or stain, the clear redwood weathers to a soft shade of gray and blends in with the surroundings. If you don't like a weathered look, a coat of sealer will preserve the rich redwood finish.

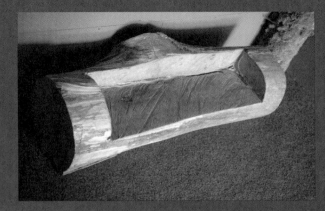

For something that really blends in with its surroundings, consider these simple benches made using just a chainsaw.

Pergola

We built this pergola for a gardener who wanted to create a garden room reminiscent of southern France or Italy. The salvaged columns were scraped down to bare wood, sanded, and varnished with several coats of polyurethane—the clear coating revealed and enhanced the inherent blemishes to give the columns an antique look. Set in the back of the garden, the pergola defines the space without enclosing it. The repetition of the roof elements creates a rhythm of light and dark as you pass underneath, and adds a strong architectural element with classical details. Planted with climbing roses or clematis, it makes a cool spot to relax and enjoy a glass of wine.

MATERIALS

- **2** 12' 4×4 #2 cedar or pressure-treated lumber *for inner ground post*
- **6** 14' 1×8 cedar *for columns*
- **6** 14' 1×6 cedar *for columns*
- **1** 6' 2×12 clear pine *for capital*

Note: pine should be treated with clear preservative for outdoor use

- **2** 12' 1⅛"×1⅝" solid crown *for capital*
- **2** 12' ¹¹⁄₁₆"×1⅛" nose cove molding *for capital*
- **2** 12' ⅞"×¹¹⁄₁₆" cove molding *for base*
- **2** 12' 1×8 pine *for base*
- **8** 80lb. bags concrete mix *for postholes*
- **6** 1¼" aluminum vents *for columns*
- **1 lb.** 3" galvanized deck screws *for columns*
- **1** 12' 6×6 cedar *for inner top posts*
- **1** 8' 6×6 cedar *for rafter supports*
- **4** 16' 2×8 cedar *for beams*
- **14** 10' 2×6 cedar *for rafters*

Installing Columns

Each column is made from four long boards joined together, with molding attached at the top and bottom. If you are going to paint your columns, you can use ordinary pine lumber provided that you first coat it with clear preservative; if you are going to let them weather naturally, use cedar, redwood, or cypress. In either case, make sure to coat the bottom and insides generously with a water sealer or preservative. A miter box is useful for making the 45-degree molding cuts.

Most columns—whether bought, homemade, or salvaged—have a hollow core, which will enable you to place the column over a pressure-treated post embedded in the ground. Make sure the dimensions of your post are smaller than the interior of the column, to allow you to make any final adjustments before cementing the column in place.

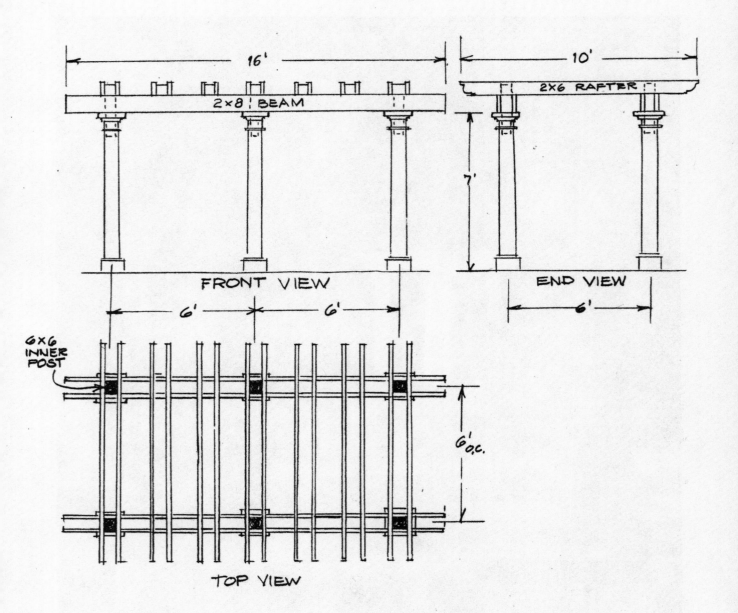

16'

2×8 BEAM

FRONT VIEW

10'

2×6 RAFTER

7'

END VIEW

6'

6'

6'

6'
O.C.

6×6
INNER
POST

TOP VIEW

45

Another example of a pergola using the same principles but with four columns and a fence to define the garden pathway.

Determine the six post locations and dig a 30"-deep hole for each post. Cut six 4×4 posts long enough for 12–16" to protrude above the ground. Align the posts so they are plumb, square, and the correct distance apart (6' on center). Backfill with soil. Pour a concrete collar 3–4" thick around the base of each post just below ground level.

Once the concrete has hardened, set the columns over the 4×4 inner posts, and secure with four 1×2 tem-porary support braces. Drill a 1⅜" vent hole through the side of the column, slightly above the inner post, and place a removable vent cap in the hole. Do not fill the columns with cement yet.

Insert a 6×6 post inside the top of each column, allowing it to protrude 12" above the top, and apply a waterproof silicone sealer to the join. Attach each col-umn securely to its inner post with a screw on each side of the column. Join the 2×8 horizontal beams

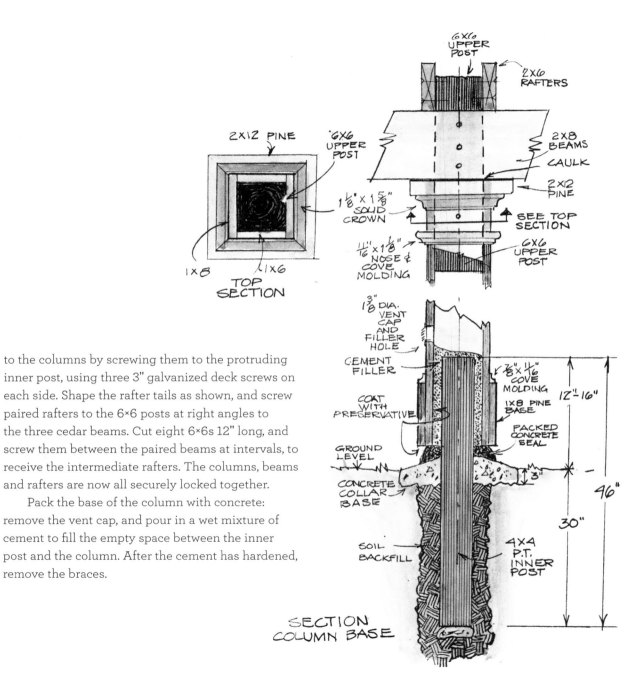

2X12 PINE

6X6 UPPER POST

1X8

1X6

TOP SECTION

6X6 UPPER POST

2X6 RAFTERS

2X8 BEAMS

CAULK

2X12 PINE

$1\frac{1}{8}" \times 1\frac{5}{8}"$ SOLID CROWN

SEE TOP SECTION

$\frac{11}{16}" \times 1\frac{1}{8}"$ NOSE & COVE MOLDING

6X6 UPPER POST

$1\frac{3}{8}"$ DIA. VENT CAP AND FILLER HOLE

CEMENT FILLER

COAT WITH PRESERVATIVE

GROUND LEVEL

CONCRETE COLLAR BASE

$\frac{7}{8}" \times \frac{11}{16}"$ COVE MOLDING

1X8 PINE BASE

PACKED CONCRETE SEAL

12"-16"

3"

46"

30"

SOIL BACKFILL

4X4 P.T. INNER POST

SECTION COLUMN BASE

to the columns by screwing them to the protruding inner post, using three 3" galvanized deck screws on each side. Shape the rafter tails as shown, and screw paired rafters to the 6×6 posts at right angles to the three cedar beams. Cut eight 6×6s 12" long, and screw them between the paired beams at intervals, to receive the intermediate rafters. The columns, beams and rafters are now all securely locked together.

Pack the base of the column with concrete: remove the vent cap, and pour in a wet mixture of cement to fill the empty space between the inner post and the column. After the cement has hardened, remove the braces.

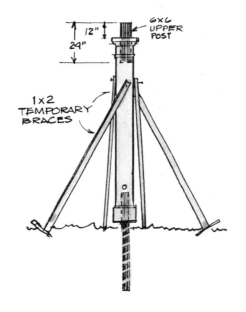

6X6
UPPER
POST

12"

29"

1X2
TEMPORARY
BRACES

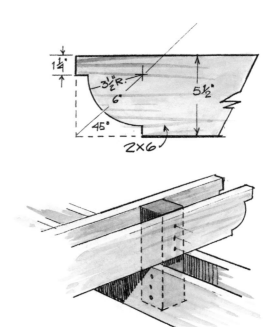

1¼"

3½"R.

6"

45°

5½"

2X6

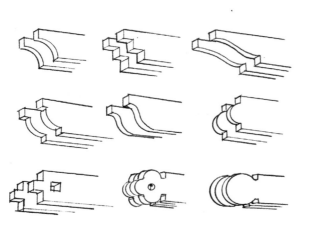

Rafter Tails

There are several different ways in which the tails, or ends, of the rafters can be cut for a more decorative appearance. Choose one of our patterns, or design your own; make a cardboard template to trace onto the ends of the rafters. Use an electric jigsaw to cut out the shapes, and sand smooth; this is time-consuming, but will add a decorative finished look to the overall design.

Rose Arbor

An arbor not only functions as an overhead support for climbing flowers or vines, but also creates a spot of shade in an otherwise sunny garden. When designing and positioning an arbor, consider both the layout of your garden and the architecture of your house. An arbor can cover a walkway or path, or it can connect a row of low shrubs or fencing. This arbor was designed to be the focus of the garden: it stands alone with no climbers planted below it, creating a formal frame for a palette of colors in the background.

MATERIALS

4	8'	4×8 clear cedar *for posts*
1		4'×8' sheet MDO plywood *for arches*
2	8'	1×4 clear cedar *for bases & capitals*
1	8'	2×4 clear cedar *for arch veneer & top slats*
1	8'	2×4 clear cedar *for crosspieces*
1		4'×4' panel clear cedar **privacy** *for lattice sides*
3	8'	2×2 clear cedar cap *for lattice sides*

16	3½" galvanized deck screws
1 lb.	2" galvanized deck screws
1 lb.	1½" galvanized finishing nails
	Epoxy glue or waterproof yellow glue
50'	Heavy hemp twine
	Coarse, medium & fine sandpaper

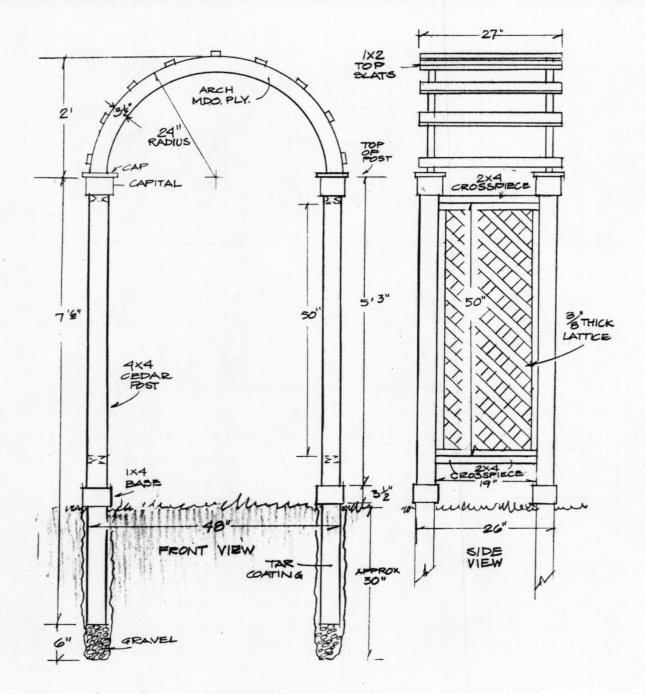

2'

3½"

ARCH
M.D.O. PLY.

24"
RADIUS

CAP
CAPITAL

TOP
OF
POST

7'6"

4×4
CEDAR
POST

50"

5'3"

1×4
BASE

3½"

48"

FRONT VIEW

TAR
COATING

APPROX
30"

6"

GRAVEL

27"

1×2
TOP
SLATS

2×4
CROSSPIECE

50"

3/8" THICK
LATTICE

2×4
CROSSPIECE
19"

26"

**SIDE
VIEW**

Posts

Cut four 4×4 cedar posts 7' long. Sand using two grades of sandpaper, and fill any holes & defects with wood filler. Using a sharp handsaw, mark and cut out a notch 3½" deep by 1½" wide from one end of each post. This is where the ends of the arches will be inserted.

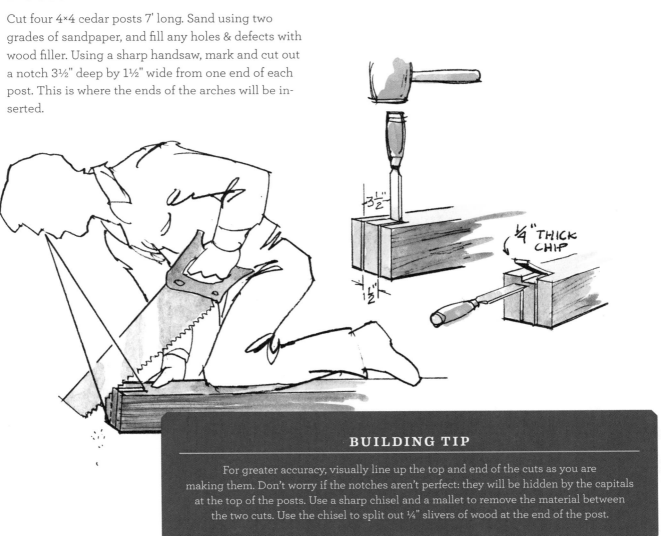

Arches

The arches are generally the most difficult section of any arbor to construct. Traditionally, they are made by cutting, clamping, and gluing many little pieces of wood together and then shaping them into a semi-circle. Our method is much easier, much stronger, less time-consuming, and has no joints: it uses MDO (medium density overlay—also called Duraply)—a weatherproof plywood originally developed for highway signs.

Each arch consists of two pieces of ¾" plywood glued together.

Lay the plywood panel on two saw-horses and mark a line lengthwise down the center. For a 48"-wide arch, mark a center point 24" from each side and from one end of the panel. Drill a ¹⁄₁₆" pivot hole through the panel at this point.

To make the curves of the arches, cut a 30"-long compass board out of 1×8. Remove the blade from your jigsaw, and trace the outline of your saw shoe (base) on the compass board, marking where the front edge of the blade fits into the shoe. Beginning at this mark, draw a line parallel to the long edge of the 1×8, and continue it to a point 24" away. This will be your pivot point. The pivot point and the front edge of the saw blade must be equidistant from the long edge of the compass board. Use the electric jigsaw (with blade reinserted!) to cut out the traced outline, to make a hole inside which the jigsaw shoe fits snugly.

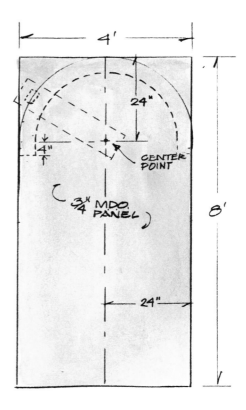

Drill a ¹⁄₁₆"-diameter hole at the pivot point, and insert a 1½" or 2" finishing nail through the compass board and the MDO panel. Use this guide to cut the arches. As you make the curved cuts, keep in mind that the tip of the saw blade will have a tendency to angle out away from the center; to prevent this, push the saw slowly along the curve, and keep the motor running at the highest speed. If your compass board is set up correctly, these curved cuts will be quite easy to make, and you should achieve a perfect semicircle every time. To cut the inside curve of the arches, make another 1/16" pivot hole 3⅜" from the first hole as shown.

Cut three more arch pieces. Stack two pieces on top of each other; check that they are exactly the same size, and glue them together with waterproof glue. Repeat with the other pair; when you're done, you should have two identical 1½"-thick arches.

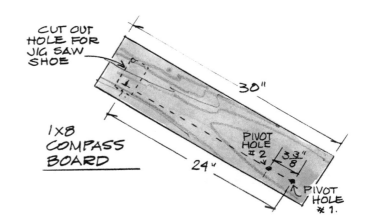

CUT OUT HOLE FOR JIG SAW SHOE

1X8 COMPASS BOARD

30"

24"

PIVOT HOLE #2

3⅜"

PIVOT HOLE #1.

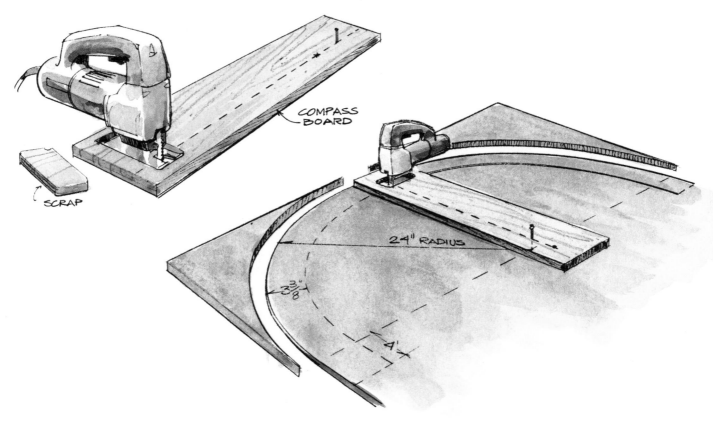

COMPASS BOARD

SCRAP

24" RADIUS

3⅜"

4'

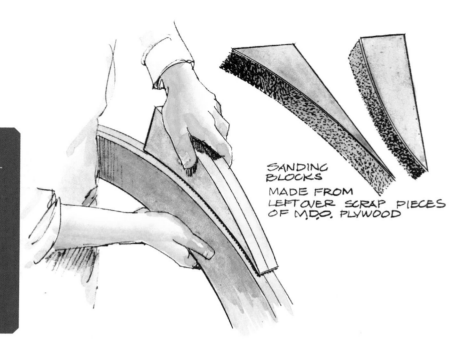

SANDING
BLOCKS
MADE FROM
LEFTOVER SCRAP PIECES
OF M.D.O. PLYWOOD

BUILDING TIP

Cut off two 11" sections from the waste pieces of MDO plywood—one from the top of the curve and one from the bottom and glue 1½"-wide coarse (60-grit) sandpaper strips to the curved edges. These sanding blocks will come in handy for smoothing the curves and eliminating flat spots.

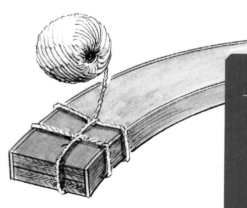

BUILDING TIP

Using a table saw, rip four ³⁄₃₂"-thick strips of clear cedar from the 8'-long 2×4. (Set aside the remaining wood for the top slats.) Glue these veneer strips to the edges of the plywood, to hide the end grain. To hold the strips in place while the glue is drying, wrap the arches with heavy hemp twine. Apply waterproof glue to all surfaces to be glued, and wrap the cord around the strips and the arch. Keep the cord pulled tightly at all times, going back under each previous turn so that the cord can be cinched up securely. There should be no gaps between the strips and the plywood arch; if there are, place wooden shims under the cord.

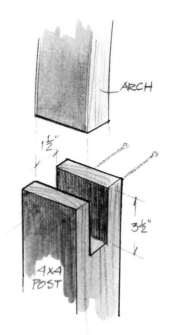

BUILDING TIP

Once the glue has dried, remove the twine and sand the edges using the corresponding sanding blocks. Fit the ends of the arch in the notched posts, gluing them in place with waterproof glue. Make sure both posts are parallel, and screw a temporary 48"-long brace across the bottom to hold them in place. Sink two 2" galvanized deck screws into each joint where the posts meet the arch.

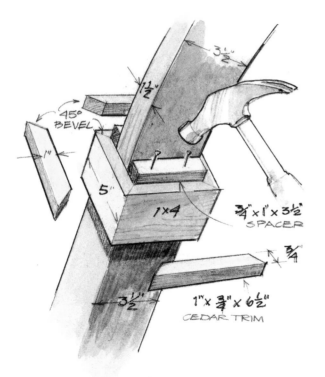

Capitals and Bases

To cover each joint where the arches meet the posts, cut four pieces of 1×4 clear cedar, about 5" long. Bevel each end and temporarily tack to the post, checking the fit. File and sand until they fit perfectly, and glue them in place. Do the same for the bottom of each post, placing the base pieces 63" from the top of the posts (see above).

To trim out the top of the capitals, cut two ¾"×1" spacers to a length of 3½" for each capital, and glue and nail them next to the face of each arch, covering the end grain of the 4×4 post. Cut four 1"×¾" clear cedar trim pieces for each capital. Miter the ends at a 45-degree angle, and glue and nail to the top of each capital (see left).

57

Crosspieces

Cut four crosspieces of clear 2×4 cedar 19" long. To attach them, counterbore two ⅜"-diameter screw holes 1½" deep in the posts. Position the screw holes below the bottom of each capital and ¾" above each base, so that the crosspieces are 50" apart. Drill the pilot holes all the way through the post, using a ³⁄₁₆"-diameter drill bit.

Lay the two sets of arches and posts on their sides, facing each other. Glue and screw the crosspieces in place, using 3½" galvanized deck screws. Once you have two crosspieces attached to one pair of posts, turn the structure over and attach the other two crosspieces.

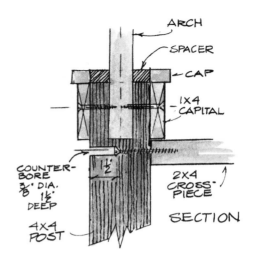

ARCH
SPACER
CAP
1X4 CAPITAL
COUNTER-BORE ⅜" DIA. 1½" DEEP
2X4 CROSS-PIECE
4X4 POST
SECTION

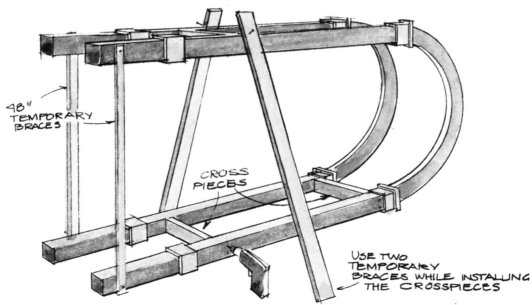

48" TEMPORARY BRACES

CROSS PIECES

USE TWO TEMPORARY BRACES WHILE INSTALLING THE CROSSPIECES

Lattice

Cut four pieces of lattice cap 19" long, and four pieces 47" long. Cut two pieces of lattice 17"×48". If you plan on painting this structure, be sure to paint the lattice and support pieces before they are assembled.

Glue all the pieces together to form a lattice frame. Fit the lattice frame into the side opening created by the crosspieces & posts, and screw in place with 2" galvanized deck screws (see side view, page 52).

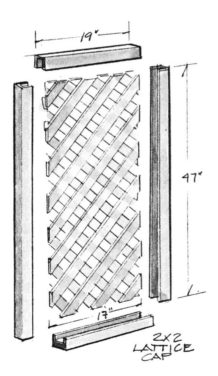

19"

47"

17"

2X2
LATTICE
CAP

Top Slats

Using the wood left over from cutting the veneer strips, rip three 8'-long pieces, each ¾" thick. Cut these into nine pieces 27" long.

Place the first two pieces 1½" up from the top of the capitals. Space the remaining pieces equally, and fasten with 2" deck screws.

Installation

To install the rose arbor, dig four 30"-deep holes, using a post hole digger. Fill the bottom of each hole with rocks or bricks (for drainage) until they are 24" deep. To protect the posts, coat the bottom 24" with roofing tar before burying them in the ground.

With an assistant, place the arbor legs in the holes and remove the temporary braces. Using a level, check that everything is plumb and level before backfilling, and tamp the dirt down with a 2×4 as you go.

Porte Couverte or "Porche"

Part of the appeal of this ornamental gate entrance is the contrast between its diminutive height and the sturdy, oversized posts supporting it. One must stoop slightly to pass under the low roof, hoping perhaps to find a child's fantasy garden beyond the gate. The space between the roof and the pickets creates a perfect frame for a vegetable or cutting garden, or even an open field.

MATERIALS

2   8'   8×8 pressure-treated lumber *for posts*

1   6'   8×8 pressure-treated lumber *for cross supports*

1   6'   4×6 pressure-treated lumber *for knee braces*

1   10'   6×6 pressure-treated lumber *for lintels*

2   8'   2×4 pressure-treated lumber *for rafters*

1   6' 2×6 pressure-treated lumber *for ridge pole*

6   12' 1×6 #2 pine *for roof sheathing*

Note: pine should be treated with clear preservative for outdoor use

1 bundle 18" hand-split cedar shakes *for roof*

2   ½"×10" lag screws *for cross support fasteners*

4   ½"×8" lag screws *for beams*

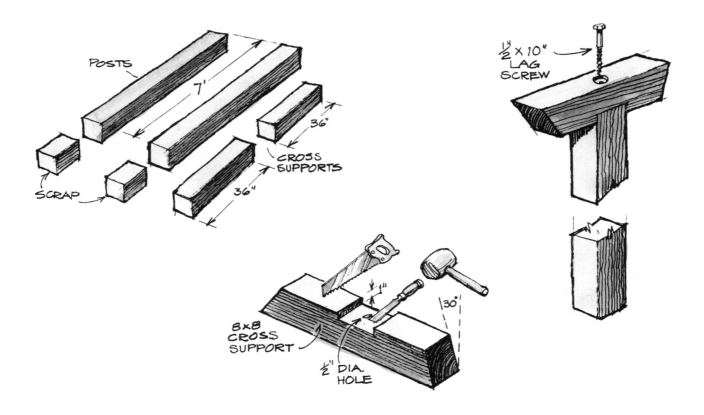

Posts & Frame

Cut the 8×8 posts and cross-supports to length: two pieces 7' long and two pieces 3' long. Cut off the ends of the cross-supports at 30-degree angles. Make a 1"-deep notch in the bottom side of the cross-supports to accept the posts.

Bore a ½"-diameter hole through the center of the notch, and attach the cross-support to the post with a 10" lag screw. Note: recess the head of the screw 1½" by counterboring first.

Dig post holes 30" deep, leaving 56" extending above ground; set the posts 32" apart. Use scrap lumber to temporarily brace the posts, making sure they are plumb and square with each other, then backfill with concrete.

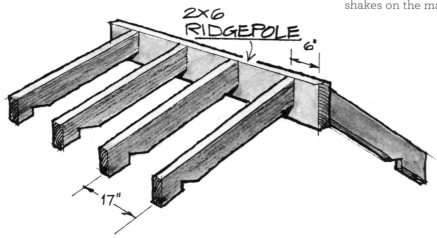

6×6 LINTEL BEAM 5'

1" DEEP NOTCHES

24"

26°

1 11/16"

2×4

1 11/16"

1 1/2"

3"

RAFTER

26°

BIRD'S MOUTH NOTCH

6 3/8"

2×6 RIDGEPOLE

6'

17"

Roof

Cut two 5' lintel beams from 6×6 lumber, and cut the ends off at 30-degree angles. Rest them on the cross-supports, and mark where they meet. Cut 1"-deep notches in the underside of the lintels beams, and screw the beams to the cross-supports, using ½"×8" lag screws recessed 1½" from the top.

Cut eight 2×4 rafters 24" long. Cut the ends off at 26 degree angles (1 11/16" from the bottom end) and cut a 1½"×3" bird's mouth notch in each.

Cut a 5' ridgepole from a 2×6. Toenail the rafters to the ridgepole and lintels 17" apart.

To build the roof, cut eight 1×6 boards 67½" long, and nail them to the rafters. Cover the boards with clay tiles or hand-split cedar shakes. "Stagger" the shakes (ensure that the joints don't line up), and double the first layer.

To cover the ridge, cut shakes 3½" wide, and weave them across the top, at right angles to the shakes on the main part of the roof.

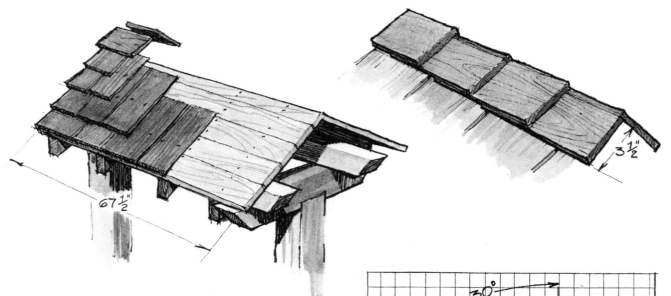

Knee Braces

To reinforce the cross supports, cut four 4×6 knee braces 16" long. A band saw is the best tool for cutting the curves, but you can use an electric jig saw with a 5" blade. Join the knee braces to the cross supports and the posts, using ⅝"-diameter wooden pegs driven through the braces and into the post.

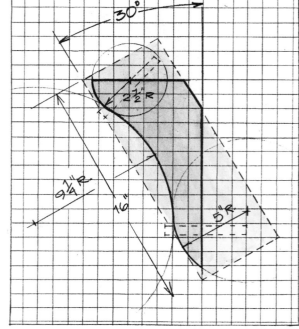

4×6 KNEE BRACE

Attach a picket gate (see *Picket Gate*, page 66)

Picket Gate

There's nothing more American than a white picket fence and gate. Mark Twain described how Tom Sawyer walked along a picket fence with a stick, clicking the fence as he went along. This simple gate should take only a morning to build. You can buy ready-cut pickets if you like; otherwise, rip and cut them from a 10'-long 1×8. Before ordering your lumber, consider what might pass through the gate (lawn mower, garden cart, or even a tractor) and therefore how wide you need to make it. To fit our Porte Couverte, reduce the width by 4".

MATERIALS

2	6' 4×4 pressure treated lumber *for posts*
2	4×4 post caps *for posts*
1	10' 1×8 clear cedar *for pickets*
1	10' 1×4 clear cedar *for diagonal & cross pieces*
1 lb.	1½" galvanized finishing nails *for diagonal & cross pieces*

2 bags	concrete
2	hinges
1	gate latch
2	handles
1 quart	exterior paint
1 can	wood putty

Cutting the Pickets

Rip-cut a 10'-long 1×8 into three equal strips; cut three 40"-long pieces from each, making a total of nine pickets. Place these on a flat work surface approximately 2" apart, and line up the edges. Temporarily nail or clamp the first end picket to the work surface so it won't move. Measure 35½" across from the outside, and temporarily nail the last picket in position, using a framing square to make sure the two are parallel. Space the remaining pickets evenly between them.

Cut two cross braces (cleats) to a length of 34". Glue and nail the cross braces to the pickets, 3" up from the bottom and 2½" down from the top of the gate. Use 1½" finishing nails, driven in at an angle so they don't stick out the other side; this also makes the nails grip better. Set them a little below the surface, using a nail set, and fill the holes with wood putty.

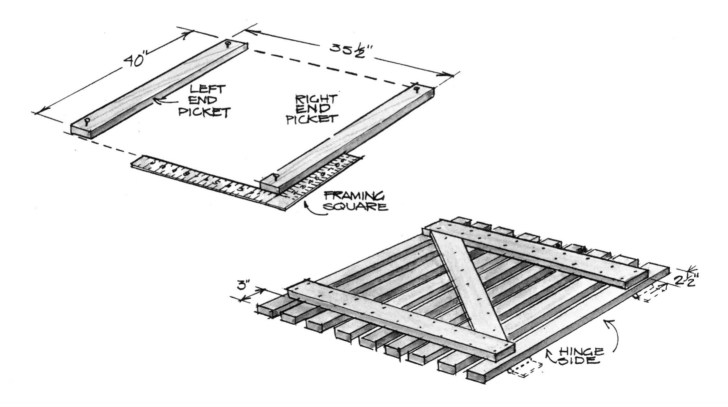

Mark where the diagonal brace will meet the two cross braces, and cut to fit. Glue and nail the brace to the top cross brace on the latch side, and to the bottom cross brace on the hinge side. Round off all exposed edges of wood, using #80 sandpaper—paint does not adhere well to sharp edges, and you don't want water to penetrate the wood.

Remove the temporary nails from the end pickets.

Installation

Cut two 6'-long posts out of 4×4 pressure-treated wood. Dig two holes, 24" deep, 39½" from center to center. Position the posts in the holes, plumb, level, and aligned with each other. Nail temporary braces to hold the posts in place.

Screw one side of each hinge to the gate. Prop up the gate next to the post, allowing ¼" clearance on each side, and screw the other half of each hinge to the post. Attach the gate handles and latch, and back-fill the holes with concrete.

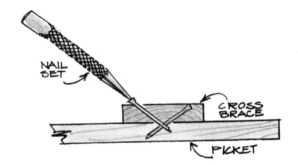

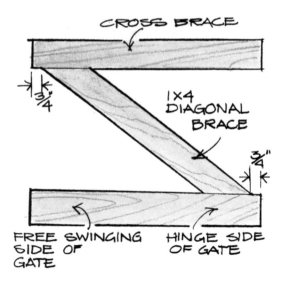

Traditional English Farm Gate

Our version of the classic five-bar gate serves as a useful introduction to the kind of joints used in full-scale timber-framing. It will suit the approach to an imposing house as well as to a field—the one we made is 9'-5" wide, but it can be any size up to, say, 12' (if you have a bigger gap than this to fill, consider having two smaller gates). The diamond bracing is very strong and eliminates the wobbliness of flimsier styles—but for a gate under about 6', a single 'X' brace is sufficient, and under 3', one diagonal will do. In the UK, we used pressure-treated wood throughout, with 3×6 uprights, a 3×4 top rail and 1×4s for the rest; a lighter gate could be made using 3×4 posts & top rail, and 1×3s elsewhere. Rough-sawn pressure-treated wood can be extremely rough, but a palm sander and router can make a big difference. You can use other kinds of wood—oak, mahogany or any local construction wood—as long as you protect it with preservative.

MATERIALS

1	8'	3×6 pressure-treated lumber *for posts*
1	10'	3×4 pressure-treated lumber *for top rail*
4	10'	1×4 pressure-treated lumber *for rails*
2	12'	1×4 pressure-treated lumber *for cross-bracing*
1	36"	1" dowel *for joints*
2		strap hinges
1		latch
16		2" bolts

The "kissing gate" traditionally allowed people (but not animals) through, provided they paid the toll—a kiss.

The post at the hinge end of our example is 48" high, the other post 1" shorter; this not only looks right but gives a subliminal hint to first-time visitors which end of the gate to aim for. We also shortened the second post by ½" at the bottom to allow for a slightly uneven driveway. The top rail is 8" below the top of the hinge post, and the other rails are spaced closer together as they descend—originally this was to keep small farm animals from wandering, but this also holds true for small pets and again, it just looks right.

Having marked the positions of the rails on the posts with a marking gauge (take extra care if they are different heights), cut the outline of the mortises with a chisel & mallet to prevent splitting. Drill out the mortise using a ¾" drill bit. We went 4¼" deep for the top and bottom rails; the others need only be 1½". All the mortises are sized to fit the 1×4s except the top one, which is 1½" wide. Clean the mortises out with the biggest chisel you can—this will make it easier to keep the sides straight. It's a nice but not essential refinement to cut a "shoulder" for the top rail. Mark and cut the tenons on the top rail to fit the mortises, cross-cutting the shoulders and removing the waste with a broad chisel. The joints should be snug but not so tight that the wood will split when forced together. Even pressure-treated wood should be treated with clear preservative wherever it has been cut; and if you do this just before assembly, it will help ease the pieces into place. Use a wooden mallet rather than a hammer if they need a little gentle persuasion. Drill through the four corners, and drive in 1" dowels or

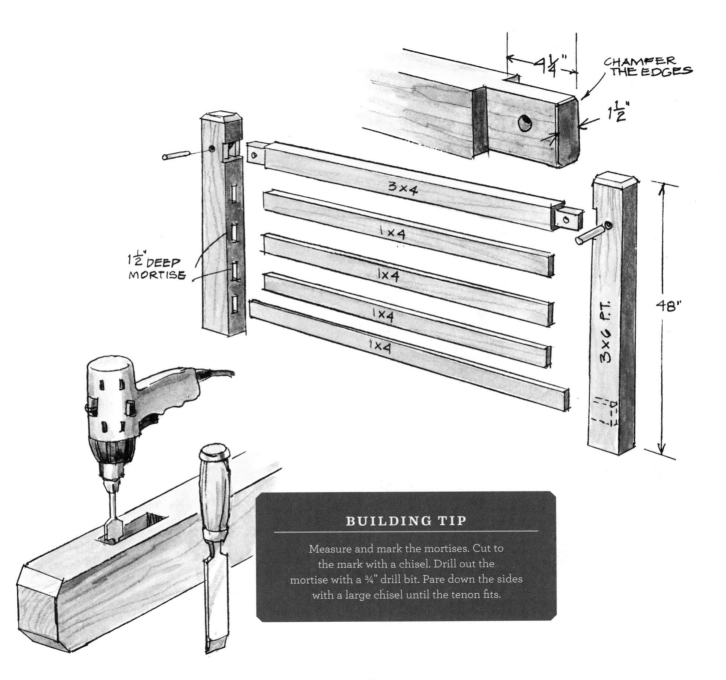

4¼"

CHAMFER
THE EDGES

1½"

3×4

1×4

1×4

1×4

1×4

1½" DEEP
MORTISE

3×6 P.T.

48"

BUILDING TIP

Measure and mark the mortises. Cut to
the mark with a chisel. Drill out the
mortise with a ¾" drill bit. Pare down the sides
with a large chisel until the tenon fits.

wooden pegs to secure the joints. Trim the dowels, taking care not to damage the surrounding wood, and sand flush.

Check that the corners are square by measuring the diagonals or with a framing square, before marking and cutting the braces. The angles will depend on the length and height of the gate. Extend the braces into the posts and top rail by chiseling out a narrow groove—no more than ⅜". Secure all intersections with 2" bolts. Use 2" countersunk screws where the braces join at the center of the top rail.

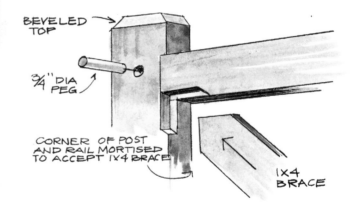

BEVELED TOP

¾" DIA PEG

CORNER OF POST AND RAIL MORTISED TO ACCEPT 1×4 BRACE

1×4 BRACE

We used three coats of clear acrylic exterior varnish (made by Polyvine) for our gate—sanding again, after the first coat had sealed the surface, to complete the transformation of the rough wood. A gate like this needs heavy strap hinges, and we also drilled a sturdy ½" bar into the closing end, to fit the heavy-duty latch that takes much of the weight when the gate is shut. It goes without saying (so we'll say it anyway) that the gate post must be rock-solid too—ours is an 8×8 pressure-treated post, set in concrete to a depth of almost 3'.

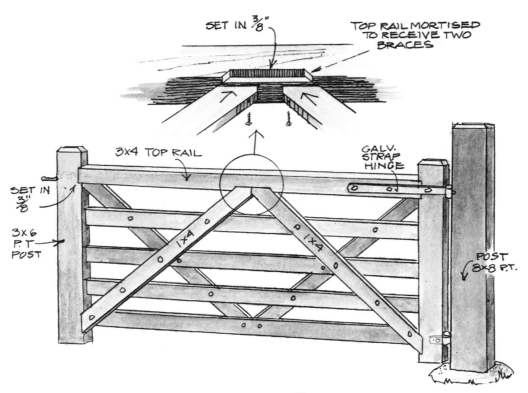

Rustic Gate

The challenge in making this gate is to find branches that will fit together. There's no list to take to the lumberyard for this project, although some nurseries or farm supply stores sell rustic poles that can be used for the posts and rails. A walk through the woods is the best way to find the raw materials, especially the more decorative inside branches that give the gate its unique personality. Pages 80 to 81 can provide some inspiration.

If possible, all parts of the branch should lie flat when it is lying on the ground. The most useful branches are forked (we call them "slingshots"). Be careful not to cut them too short—save the final trimming for later. Always gather twice as many branches as you think you will need. The best type of wood is hickory or juniper, but cedar will work too. Start with straight branches, for the vertical posts and horizontal rails. For a 36"-wide gate, the posts should be about 3" in diameter, the rails slightly less. The inside branches should measure ½" to 1½" in diameter. Gates that span a larger distance need to be correspondingly more substantial.

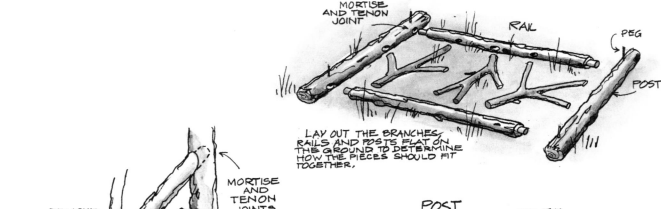

MORTISE AND TENON JOINT

RAIL

PEG

POST

LAY OUT THE BRANCHES, RAILS AND POSTS FLAT ON THE GROUND TO DETERMINE HOW THE PIECES SHOULD FIT TOGETHER.

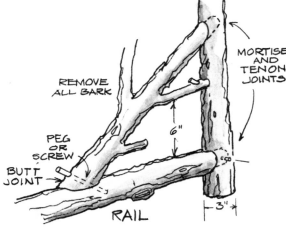

REMOVE ALL BARK

MORTISE AND TENON JOINTS

PEG OR SCREW

BUTT JOINT

6"

3"

RAIL

GLUE ALL JOINTS WITH EPOXY

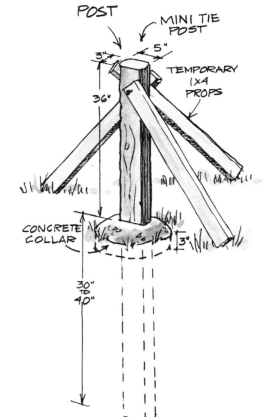

POST

MINI TIE POST

TEMPORARY 1×4 PROPS

3"

5"

36"

CONCRETE COLLAR

3"

30" TO 40"

Bury two strong posts, one on either side of the gate opening, allowing for ½" clearance on each side of the gate. For a small gate, "mini landscape ties" are a good choice: these are inexpensive pressure-treated 5×3s, 8' long with two rounded faces. Using a shovel or posthole digger, dig two holes 30"–48" deep (depending on your frost line). Place the posts in the holes and hold them vertical by nailing three short props to the posts. Backfill and tamp the soil down using a spare 2×4, and finish with a 3"-thick concrete collar at the grade level. Allow 24 hours for the concrete to harden.

Remove all bark from the branches.

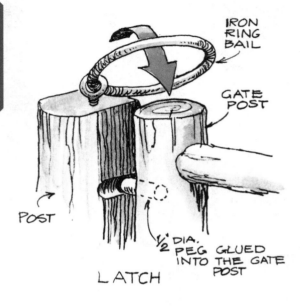

To make the gate frame, join the pieces together by first drilling 1"-deep holes into the posts to accept the rails. These holes should be slightly smaller than the rails, and the rails shaved off to fit. Use epoxy to glue the rails into the posts, and secure them with a screw or peg.

Once the glue has dried, lay the frame on the ground and arrange the other branches for the best effect. Try to place the pieces about 6" apart. Start with the largest branches and mark where they will join the posts and rails. Cut each branch about 1" longer than the gap it is filling, to allow for the joint. Only one end of the branch can be mortised; the other end will be butted to the rail or post. Carve and shape the ends to fit snugly, before drilling, gluing, and pegging them in place. The gate should look as though it had grown into this shape on its own.

For a simple hinge, screw 2"-long stainless-steel eye bolts into the post and the gate, rest the gate on the post bolts and attach ⅜"×1½" bolts and washers through both eye bolts. This hinge allows the gate to open either inwards or outwards.

To hold the gate closed, drill a ½"-diameter hole in the post and another in the gate. Insert a rounded ½" peg in the gate hole. Since there is some flexibility in the hinges, the peg will slide into the hole when the gate swings shut. For a more secure closure, you can add an iron ring that flips over the gatepost.

Found wood and oddly shaped pieces can be used for all sorts of outdoor projects, furniture, and sculpture. We saw these at Heligan and Trelissick in Cornwall, UK, and Richmond, Virginia

2

Sheds and Outdoor Spaces

Here you'll find everything from the most practical backyard workrooms for the handyman, the gardener, or the artist, to more elaborate & decorative designs combining usefulness with elegance to add interest, character & individuality to a garden or backyard.

Garden Shower

There's nothing like showering outside for cleaning up and cloud watching. Open-air showering provides a wonderful way to get the sand off your feet after a day at the beach, or to relax after a morning's work in the garden or potting shed. The front of the garden shower makes a great backdrop for flowers or greenery, such as brightly colored annuals or a fragrant rosebush surrounded by ivy. The plants will thrive on being watered regularly!

MATERIALS

5	8'	**4×4 pressure-treated lumber** *for frame posts*
1	6'	**2×4 cedar** *for side frame*
1	10'	**2×4 cedar** *for front frame*
15	8'	**1×6 clear cedar tongue & groove** *for door, front & sides*
1	12'	**1×4 #2 cedar** *for top trim*
2	8'	**1×6 cedar** *for cap trim*
1	14'	**1×6 #2 cedar** *for front panel trim*
2	10'	**1×6 #2 cedar** *for door battens, braces & trim*
1	12'	**1×4 cedar** *for seat*

5	10'	**⁵⁄₄×4 redwood or pressure-treated decking** *for floor decking & seat cleats*
1	12'	**2×4 pressure-treated lumber** *for floor joists*
2		**3½" galvanized self-closing hinges** *for door*
1		**6" thumb latch** *for door*
1 lb.		**2" galvanized finishing nails**
1 lb.		**1¼" galvanized deck screws**
6		**⅜"×6" lag screws with washers**
1	3'	**1"-diameter wooden dowel** *for pegboard*

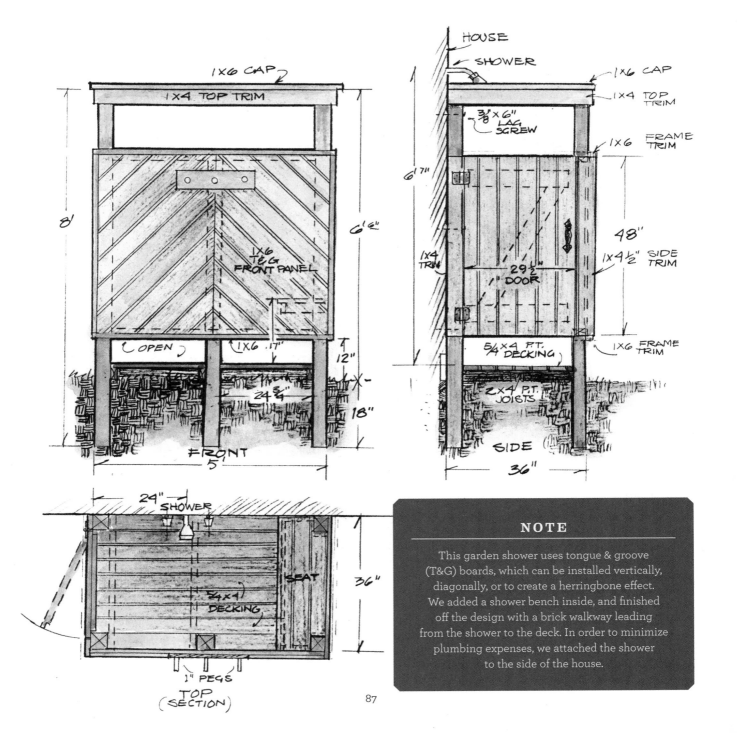

1X6 CAP

1X4 TOP TRIM

1X6 CAP

8'

6'6"

1X6 T&G
FRONT PANEL

OPEN

1X6 17"

12"

24¾"

18"

FRONT

5'

HOUSE

SHOWER

1X6 CAP

1X4 TOP TRIM

⅜" X 6"
LAG SCREW

1X6 FRAME TRIM

6'7"

1X4 TRIM

29½"
1" DOOR

48"

1X4½" SIDE TRIM

5/4 X 4 P.T.
DECKING

1X6 FRAME TRIM

2X4 P.T.
JOISTS

SIDE

36"

24" SHOWER

5/4 X 4
DECKING

SEAT

36"

1" PEGS

TOP
(SECTION)

NOTE

This garden shower uses tongue & groove (T&G) boards, which can be installed vertically, diagonally, or to create a herringbone effect. We added a shower bench inside, and finished off the design with a brick walkway leading from the shower to the deck. In order to minimize plumbing expenses, we attached the shower to the side of the house.

87

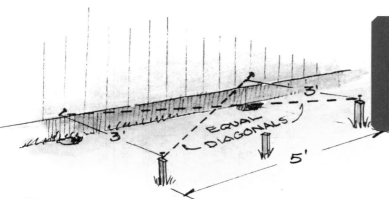

Frame

The shower is built on five sturdy 4×4 posts. Measure and mark where the first two post holes will be dug against the side of the house—they should be 5' apart and 18" deep. Measure out 3' from the first two post holes, and set two stakes 5' apart. Check that the stakes are square with the house by measuring diagonally. Both measurements should be the same (approximately 70"). Cut a third stake and center it between the two front stakes. Remove all three stakes and in their place, dig three 18"-deep holes. Cut a 78"-long 4×4 center post, and place this in its hole. Place an 8'-long 4×4 in each of the other holes. Do not backfill until later.

Attach the first two posts to the house using ⅜"×6" lag screws (assuming it's a wooden wall).

To connect and trim out the tops of the posts, cut a 61½"-long piece of 1×4, and nail it to the top front of the front two corner posts. Leave a ¾" overhang at each end. Cut two more 1×4 boards, each 36" long, and nail them to the top sides, spanning the distance between the posts attached to the house and the front two corner posts.

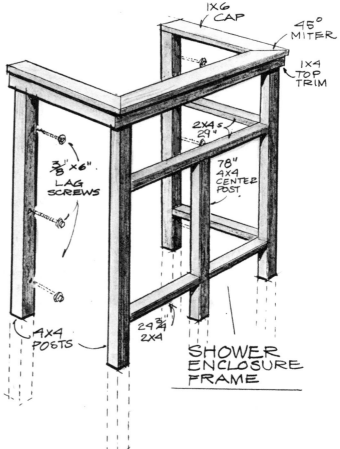

SHOWER ENCLOSURE FRAME

Cap the tops of the corner posts and trim pieces with 1×6 boards laid flat, and with 45-degree miters at the front outside corners of the shower enclosure.

To frame the top of the front panel, cut a 53"-long piece of 2×4, toenail it between the two front corner posts 5' up from the ground, and nail it to the top of the center post.

To frame the bottom of the front panel, cut two pieces of 2×4, 24¾" long, and toenail them between the front corner posts and the center post 12" up from the ground. Toenail two more 2×4s 29" long between the two side posts opposite the doorway. Check that the structure is square & plumb, and backfill the holes.

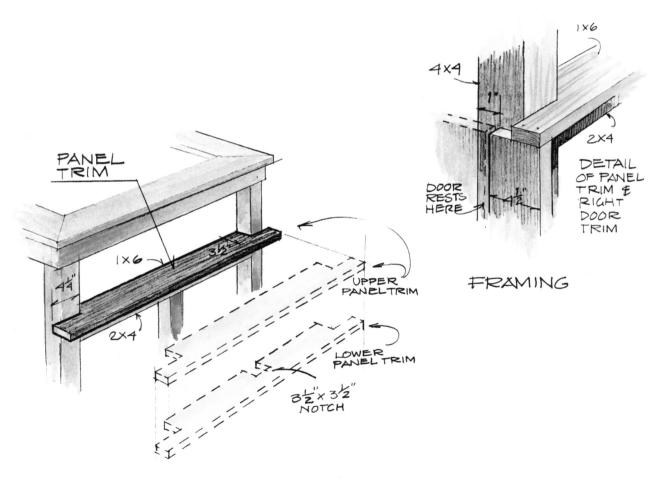

PANEL TRIM

1×6

4¼"

2×4

3½" × 3½" NOTCH

UPPER PANEL TRIM

LOWER PANEL TRIM

4×4

1"

1×6

2×4

DOOR RESTS HERE

½"

DETAIL OF PANEL TRIM & RIGHT DOOR TRIM

FRAMING

Panels and Trim

Cover the front of the shower enclosure with 1×6 T&G cedar: cut the ends off at 45-degree angles and nail diagonally to the posts and horizontal frame.

Cover the right side of the shower enclosure with vertical 1×6 T&G boards, overlapping the front diagonal boards by 1".

To trim the frame of the front panel, attach 1×6s 61½" long to the top and bottom of the panel. Cut a 3½"×4½" notch at each end of the trim, to fit around the corner posts; notch out the middle of the bottom piece of 1×6 for the center post.

In preparation for hanging the door, rip cut two 4'-long pieces of 1×6 T&G, one 3½" wide and another 4½" wide. These will be the left and right trim pieces. Nail the right trim piece in place, overlapping the front panel by 1" and making it flush with the front panel trim. Temporarily nail the left trim to the post attached to the house. The distance between the two pieces of trim should be approximately 30".

Door and Seat

Join together six 4'-long pieces of 1×6 T&G. Rip cut the left and right boards square so that the total width of the six pieces measures about 29½". Cut two 1×6 battens 28¼" long, and screw them to the backs of the boards, 4" from top and bottom, using 1¼" galvanized screws. Place another 1×6 diagonally across the door, with the ends overlapping the battens. Mark the diagonal brace where it meets the battens, and cut to fit. Attach the brace to the back of the door.

Screw two 3½" galvanized self-closing hinges 5" from the top and bottom of the door, and screw the door to the left trim piece and post.

Install a thumb latch (operable from either side), and a hook & eye for privacy on the inside of the door.

Build a 36"-wide seat from ⁵⁄₄×4 cedar. For the seat top, cut three pieces 36" long and one piece 29" long. Cut two cleats 7" long and two 3½" long. Nail them to the house wall, front panel & side posts. Nail the front of the seat to the front edge of the 7" cleats, and nail the top pieces to the side cleats, using 2" galvanized finishing nails.

Build an optional ledge for soap and shampoo out of a 1×4, toenailed between two of the front posts.

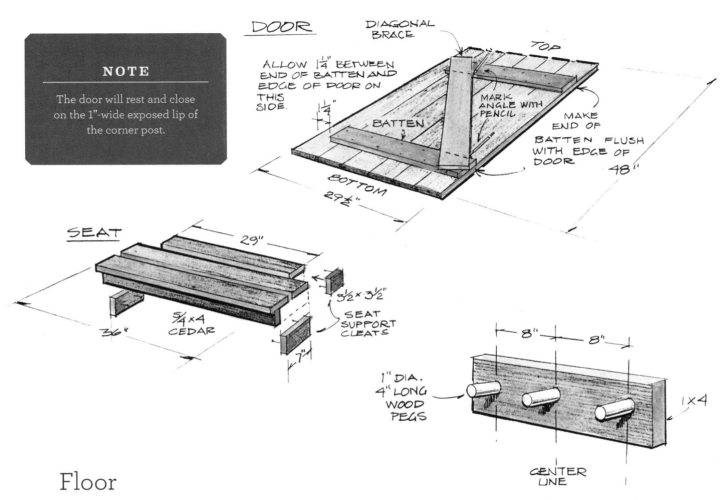

NOTE

The door will rest and close on the 1"-wide exposed lip of the corner post.

DIAGONAL BRACE

ALLOW 1¼" BETWEEN END OF BATTEN AND EDGE OF DOOR ON THIS SIDE.

1¼"

BATTEN

TOP

MARK ANGLE WITH PENCIL

MAKE END OF BATTEN FLUSH WITH EDGE OF DOOR

48"

BOTTOM 29½"

SEAT

29"

5⁄4×4 CEDAR

36"

3½ × 3½"

SEAT SUPPORT CLEATS

7"

8" 8"

1" DIA. 4" LONG WOOD PEGS

1×4

CENTER LINE

Floor

Cut three floor joists 36" long out of 2×4 P.T. lumber, and nail them to the bottom of the posts inside the shower stall (see section view, page 87). Attach a rail across the two back posts to support the end of the center joist. Check that they are level in all directions. Cut 7 pieces of 5⁄4×4 P.T. lumber 5' long, and screw them to the joists using 1½" galvanized deck screws. Cut a piece of 5⁄4×4 P.T. lumber 53" long to fit between the back posts, and two 24¾"-long pieces to fit between the front and center posts. Screw them in place.

As a final touch, build a pegboard from a 2×4, about 21" long. Drill a 1"-diameter hole in the center and 2 additional holes, 8" from the center peg. Cut three 6"-pieces of 1"-diameter dowel, and glue them into the holes. Screw the pegboard to the center of the front panel, 6" down from the top.

Garden Kiosk

This elegant garden tool house serves as a convenient storage place for garden tools, while also providing a decorative focal point for your garden. Add to the effect with a brick or stone path leading up to it. You can run a water line to it with a spigot and a raised stand to avoid the inconvenience and unsightly mess of dragging a garden hose back and forth from the house. As an optional feature, consider turning the top into a birdhouse.

MATERIALS

2	4'×8'	¾" exterior AC plywood *for box and floor*
1	4'×8'	⅜" exterior AC plywood *for door and trim*
1	10'	1×8 *for base*
1	10'	1×4 *for base trim*
1	10'	1×3 *for base trim*
1	8'	¹¹⁄₁₆"×¹¹⁄₁₆" cove molding *for base trim*
1	8'	⅝"×1⅝" bull nose *for base trim*
1	4'×8'	⅛" privacy trellis *for sides and back*
1	12'	1×10 #2 pine *for molding support*

Note: pine should be treated with clear preservative for outdoor use

1	12'	¹¹⁄₁₆"×5¼" sprung *for cornice molding and crown molding*

2	12'	⅜"×1½" bull nose molding *for cornice molding*
1	12'	⁹⁄₁₆"×2⅝" cove molding *for cornice molding*
1	12'	¾" half-round molding *for top panel edge*
1	12'	2×6 #2 construction fir *for rafters*
1½	4'×8'	¼" exterior AC plywood *for roof*
1		5"-diameter wood finial ball *for roof finial*

Titebond II glue

1 box 1" galvanized wire nails

3 1"×3" butt hinges

1 5" thumb latch

1 box 1½" galvanized finishing nails

1 quart exterior paint

1 box 2" galvanized finishing nails

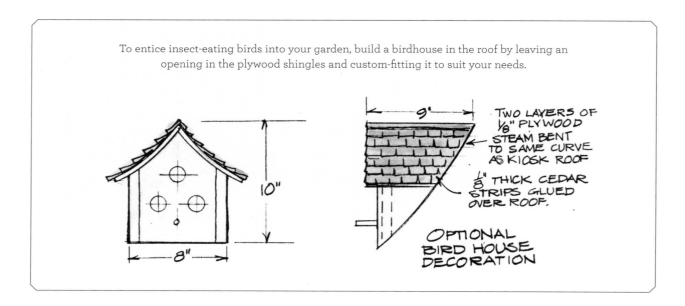

To entice insect-eating birds into your garden, build a birdhouse in the roof by leaving an opening in the plywood shingles and custom-fitting it to suit your needs.

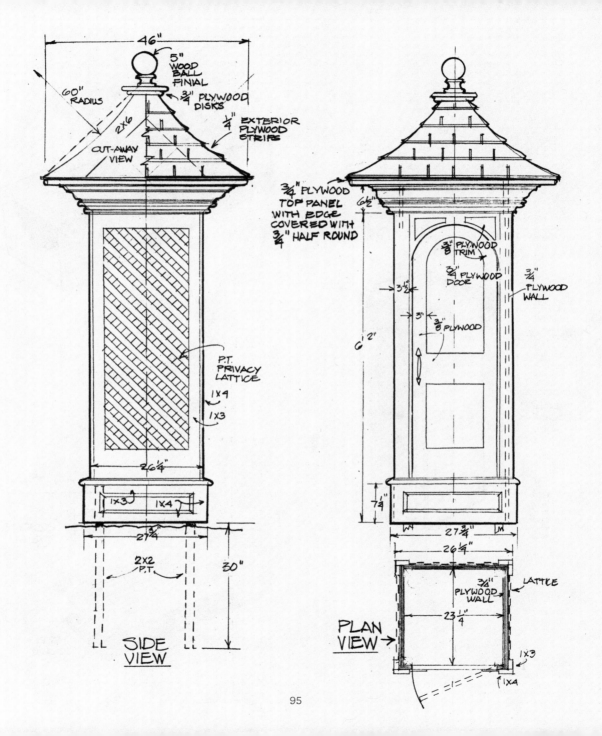

46"

5"
WOOD
BALL
FINAL

3/4" PLYWOOD
DISKS

60" RADIUS

2×6

CUT-AWAY VIEW

1/4" EXTERIOR PLYWOOD STRIPS

P.T. PRIVACY LATTICE

1×4

1×3

26 1/4"

1×3   1×4

27 3/4"

2×2 P.T.

30"

SIDE VIEW

3/4" PLYWOOD TOP PANEL WITH EDGE COVERED WITH 3/4" HALF ROUND

6 1/2"

3/8" PLYWOOD TRIM

3/4" PLYWOOD DOOR

3/4" PLYWOOD WALL

3 1/2"

6' 2"

3"

3/8" PLYWOOD

7 1/4"

27 3/4"

26 1/4"

3/4" PLYWOOD WALL

LATTICE

23 1/4"

1×3

1×4

PLAN VIEW

Sides

Begin by cutting two 4'×8' sheets of ¾" exterior plywood in half lengthwise. Cut four pieces 80½" long. Glue and screw the four pieces together so that you end up with a 24¾"×24¾"-square box.

To make the door, start by measuring in 3" from each side of the front. Draw a semi-circular 9⅜" radius arc. Carefully cut out the door using an electric jigsaw.

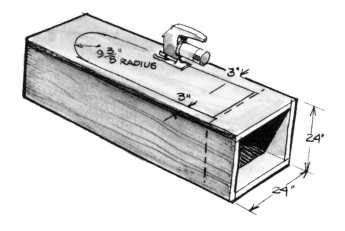

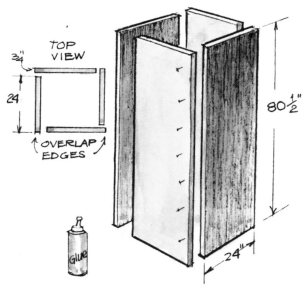

Door Trim

Trace the door onto a piece of ⅜" exterior plywood and mark the openings. Cut out the door trim; glue and clamp it to the plywood door. Cut out the corner trim pieces from leftover ⅜" plywood.

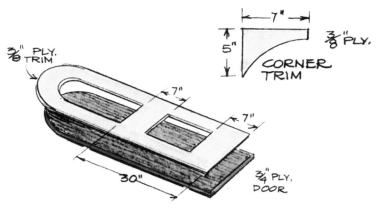

Floor

Cut a piece of ¾" plywood 23¼" square. Using scrap pieces of lumber for support, glue and screw the floor in place, 7¼" up from the bottom of the box.

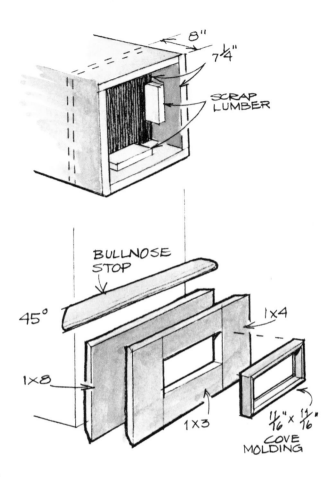

Base Trim

Measure the outside perimeter of the base and cut four 1×8 boards to fit around it. Glue and nail the boards to the bottom. Cut pieces of 1×4 and 1×3 to frame the 1×8 boards and glue in place. Cut four pieces of ¹¹⁄₁₆"× ¹¹⁄₁₆" cove molding to fit inside the 1×4 and 1×3 frames. Cut a ⅝"×1⅝" bull nose stop to cover the top of the base. Miter the corners at 45-degrees, and glue and nail in place using 1" galvanized wire nails and waterproof glue.

HANGING DOORS

It is easier to hang a lightweight door if you first screw the hinges to the door & door trim (casing), then attach the trim to the doorway. Attach a handle to the door to give you something to hold onto while you are installing it. Support the bottom of the door with the toe of your boot and, when you are sure it is aligned properly, nail the door trim onto the siding.

Door

Hang the door on three 1×3 hinges, leaving a ⅛" gap on each side. Screw a 5" handle with a thumb latch on to the door.

Back and Sides

Cover the corners of the box with a combination of 1×3s, 1×4s, and ⅛" lattice. Make a rabbet cut on the back of each piece of trim—this makes a lip to hold the lattice in place. Cut three pieces of ⅛" privacy lattice to cover the sides and back of the kiosk, and fit inside the lip of the trim. Secure the lattice by attaching the trim over it, using 2" galvanized finishing nails.

Molding Support

To provide a flat surface for the moldings, bevel out a 10" wide board, 45 degrees on edge. Make a compound miter cut at each end so that the boards will fit together at the corners. Cut a 46" square out of ¾" plywood, and screw it to the top of the box. Screw the molding support boards to the top panel and the box walls. Cut, glue, and nail ¾" half-round molding to the edges of the top panel.

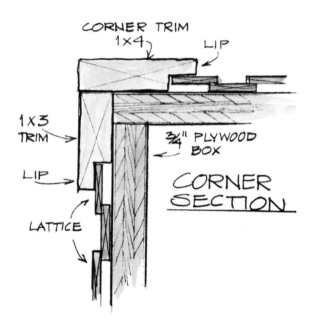

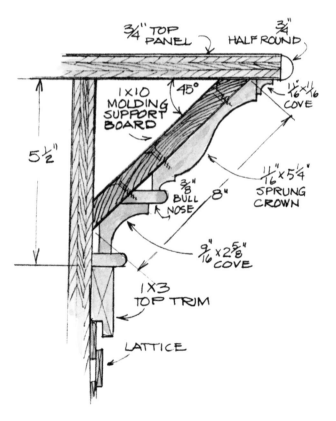

¾" HALF ROUND MOLDING

TOP PANEL

MOLDING SUPPORT BOARD

Cornice Molding

A simple cutting jig will help you cut the cornice molding accurately. Join two 3' lengths of 2×6 at right angles.

Screw a ¾"-square strip of wood to hold the bottom of the molding when you cut it. Reposition the strip to accommodate the different sizes of molding. Using the miter box, cut and fit all the pieces to size.

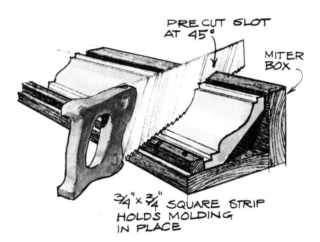

PRE CUT SLOT AT 45°

MITER BOX

¾" x ¾" SQUARE STRIP HOLDS MOLDING IN PLACE

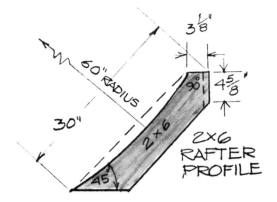

3 1/8"

60" RADIUS

30"

90°

4 5/8"

2×6

45

2×6
RAFTER
PROFILE

Rafters

Cut four 30⅜"-long pieces of 2×6. Draw a 60"-radius curve on one side of each piece, and cut out the pieces using an electric jigsaw. Cut the bottoms of the rafters at 45-degree angles. Cut the tops as shown (see left). You will need to cut ¾" off one pair of rafters so they fit together in the center.

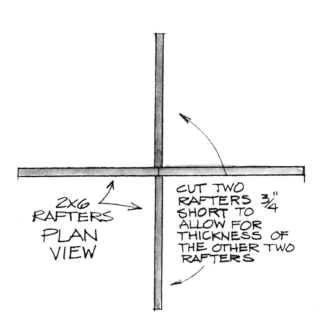

2×6
RAFTERS
PLAN
VIEW

CUT TWO
RAFTERS 3¾"
SHORT TO
ALLOW FOR
THICKNESS OF
THE OTHER TWO
RAFTERS

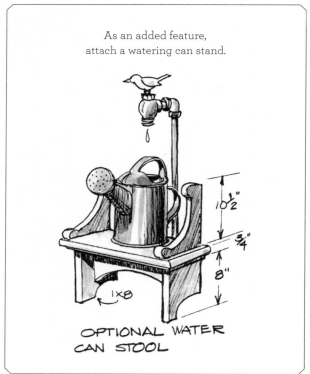

As an added feature,
attach a watering can stand.

10 ½"

¾"

8"

1×8

OPTIONAL WATER
CAN STOOL

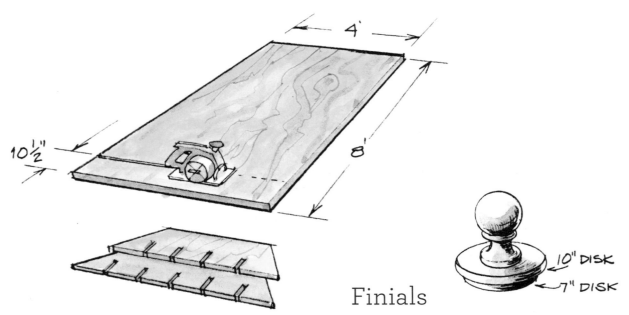

Roof Shingles

From 1½ sheets of 4'×8' ¼" exterior plywood, cut boards 10½" wide. Measure and cut each board, to fit the rafters and to make five overlapping rows. Before attaching, cut notches in the bottom edges to simulate shingles. Attach the boards to the rafters, using construction adhesive and 2" galvanized finishing nails.

Finials

Cut two ¾" plywood disks, one 7" in diameter and the other 10" in diameter. Glue and screw them to the top of the rafters. Top off with a 5"-diameter wooden ball.

> **NOTE**
>
> Hang the most frequently used tools on the inside of the door, and use the inside back wall to hang heavier tools such as shovels and spades.

Hexagonal Garden House

Elegant and well suited to a formal garden, this classic garden shed was inspired by a colonial garden shed built for George Washington's home in Mount Vernon, Virginia. It looks beautiful in a country garden, or in the backyard of a city brownstone or townhouse. Six feet wide, it is large enough to store all the essential tools for your garden and still leave plenty of room for kids to disappear in when playing hide-and-seek. We adapted this design for a small New York City backyard, turning it into a 5-sided shed to fit into a corner. (See photo on page 105).

MATERIALS

3 12' 2×6 pressure-treated lumber *for base & floor joists*

1 2' 2×6 pressure-treated lumber *for windowsill*

2 4'×8' ¾" exterior plywood *for floor deck*

6 8×8×8 concrete half blocks *for base*

2 or 3 assorted gray slates *for shims*

3 12' 4×4 pressure-treated lumber or cedar posts *for corners*

4 10' 2×4 #2 fir *for plates*

Note: fir & pine should be treated with clear preservative for outdoor use

2 8' 2×2 clear cedar *for window sash*

1 6' 1×6 cedar *for window jamb*

2 10' 2×4 #2 construction fir nailers *for wall framing*

22 12' 1×6 tongue & groove #2 cedar *for siding & door*

4 12' 1×2 cedar *for dentils & bevel support strip*

2 12' 4½" sprung crown molding *for cornice*

2 10' 1×6 #2 pine *for crown support*

1 10' 2×4 #2 construction fir *for temporary post*

3 10' 2×6 #2 construction fir *for rafters*

3 4'×8' ½" exterior plywood *for roof*

1 roll 36" #15 roofing felt *for roof*

3 bundles 36" three-tab asphalt shingles *for roof*

1 12' 1×2 #2 cedar *for doorstops*

1 12' ⁵⁄₄×6 pressure-treated lumber *for door cross braces & head jamb*

1 12' ⁵⁄₄×4 #2 pine *for door casing*

Hardware

1lb. 1½" galvanized deck screws *for door*

1lb. 3½" galvanized deck screws

1lb. 2" galvanized deck screws

3lbs. 2" spiral- or ring-shank siding nails

2 2" galvanized hinges

1 dozen 1½" copper nails

2 18" wrought-iron strap hinges

1 24"×24" 16oz. copper sheet

1 9½"×21½" window glass

Waterproof yellow glue

1 thumb latch

Base

Cut six 36"-long pieces of 2×6 pressure-treated lumber and, using a portable circular saw, bevel cut each end at a 30-degree angle.

Assemble the pieces on a flat surface and screw the corners together using 3½" deck screws at each joint. Check that the opposite corners are exactly 6' apart.

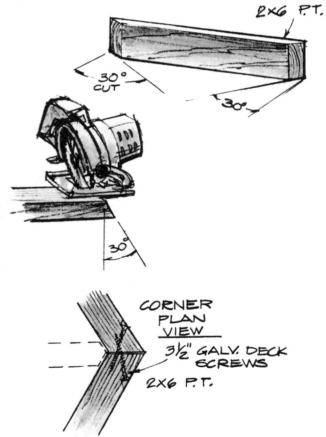

Cut three 6'-long pieces of 2×6 P.T. lumber for the floor joists. Cut the ends of the first piece (cross joist) to fit into two opposite corners of the base. The next two pieces must be cut in half and shaped to fit the first piece where they intersect at the center. Screw them in place using four 3½" deck screws at each joint.

To build the plywood floor, lay the floor frame over one sheet of ¾" exterior plywood and trace the outline onto the plywood. Do the same to the other

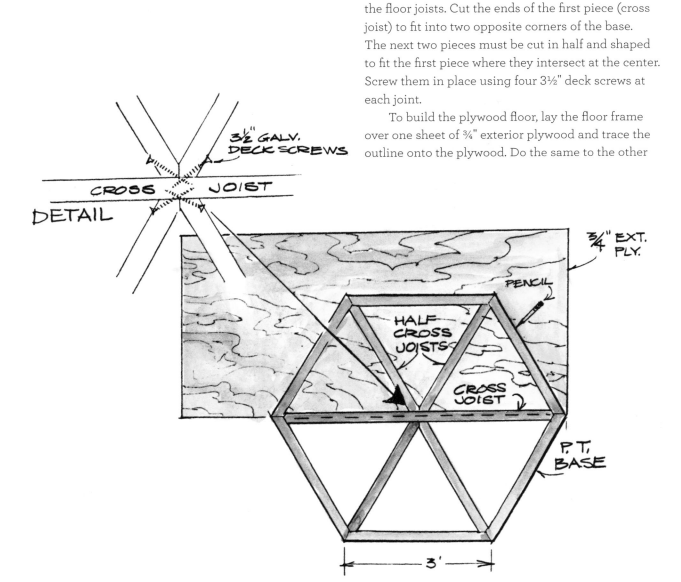

3½" GALV. DECK SCREWS

CROSS JOIST

DETAIL

¾" EXT. PLY.

PENCIL

HALF CROSS JOISTS

CROSS JOIST

P.T. BASE

3'

side, and use an electric jigsaw to cut out the two pieces of plywood. Nail the plywood to the base, using 2" spiral- or ring-shank nails.

Check the level from time to time during construction, as the soil may compress unevenly. You can use slate shims to make adjustments if necessary. Slate is sold expressly for this purpose at most lumberyards. Split off thin pieces with a claw hammer.

Wall Framing

This garden house has a 4×4 post at each corner. To provide a good nailing surface for the siding, rip two adjacent edges of each post at 30-degree angles. Cut the posts 68½" long and screw them to the base. Connect the tops of the posts with 2×4 top plates laid flat. Cut each 2×4 36" long, and miter the ends at 60 degrees. Screw them to the tops of the posts. Use a level and a framing square to make sure the structure is level, plumb and square.

Add a second layer of 2×4s (cap plates) over the top wall plate, so it overhangs by ¾". The cap plate will cover the top of the siding, and act as a solid base

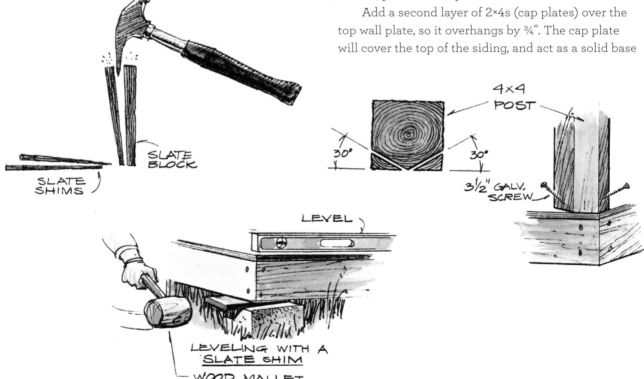

SLATE BLOCK

SLATE SHIMS

LEVEL

LEVELING WITH A SLATE SHIM

WOOD MALLET

4×4 POST

30°   30°

3½" GALV. SCREW

for the dentils. Cut these pieces off at a 60-degree angle. They will be longer (approximately 38" along the outside edge) than the top plates because they extend out further.

Frame the window and the door using 2×4s. Measure and cut the studs to fit between the bottom of the top plate and the plywood floor.

Cut 2×4 nailers (cats) to fit between all the studs and corner posts. Screw them to the studs and posts, 36" up from the floor.

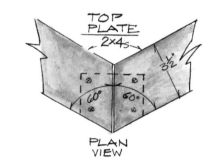

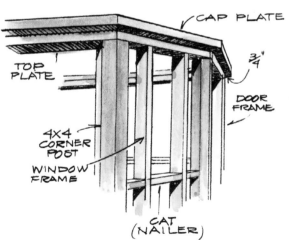

Window

This 1'-wide window is worth the effort: it's exactly this kind of extravagance that lends quality to the design and makes this structure so elegant.

You can order ready-made windows from your lumberyard, but making your own gives individuality to the design. The one shown here is very inexpensive and quick to make if you have access to a table saw. It uses only one piece of glass instead of several small panes—the muntins are applied to both sides of the glass (or plastic) to give the impression of true divided lites.

Use a table saw to cut out the four pieces for the window sash from 2×2 clear cedar. The two long sides (stiles) are 24" long, the short pieces (rails) 12". Cut 45-degree bevels on each end.

Locate the center points where the muntin bars will join the frame, and cut ⅝"×⅜" dadoes.

To hold the window glass, make a ⅛"-wide by ⅜"-deep groove down the center of each inside face of the sash. Fit a piece of ⅛" glass into the groove. (Most hardware stores or picture framers will cut glass to size.)

For the muntin bars, cut a piece of 2×2 in quarters with a table saw, so that you have four ⅝"-square lengths. Make sure they fit the dadoes.

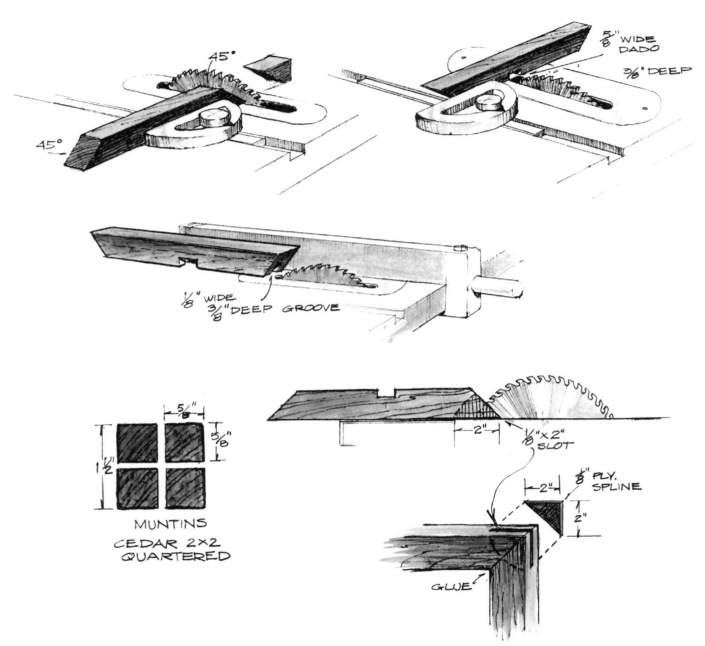

45°

45°

$\frac{5}{8}$" WIDE
DADO

$\frac{3}{8}$" DEEP

$\frac{1}{8}$" WIDE
$\frac{3}{8}$" DEEP GROOVE

$\frac{5}{8}$"

$\frac{5}{8}$"

$1\frac{1}{2}$"

MUNTINS
CEDAR 2×2
QUARTERED

2"

$\frac{1}{8}$"×2"
SLOT

$\frac{1}{8}$" PLY.
SPLINE

2"

2"

GLUE

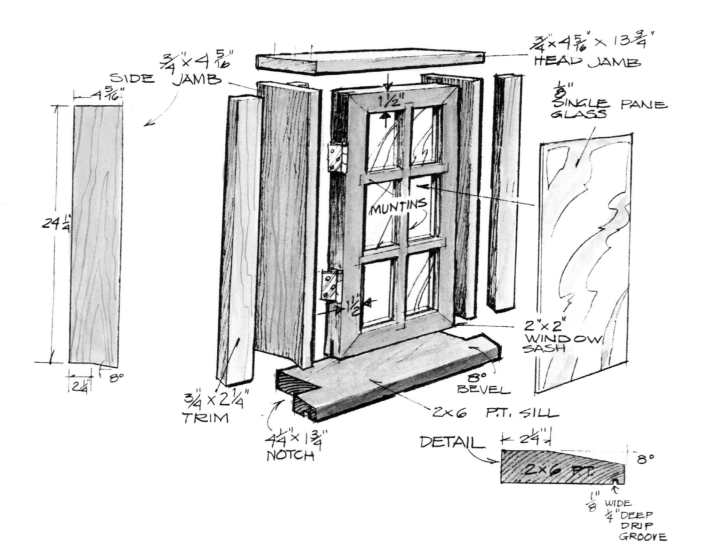

SIDE JAMB
$\frac{3}{4}"\times 4\frac{5}{16}"$

$4\frac{5}{16}"$

$24\frac{1}{4}"$

$2\frac{1}{4}"$

$8°$

HEAD JAMB
$\frac{3}{4}"\times 4\frac{5}{16}"\times 13\frac{3}{4}"$

$\frac{1}{8}"$ SINGLE PANE GLASS

$1\frac{1}{2}"$

MUNTINS

$1\frac{1}{2}"$

2"×2" WINDOW SASH

TRIM
$\frac{3}{4}"\times 2\frac{1}{4}"$

NOTCH
$4\frac{1}{4}"\times 1\frac{3}{4}"$

$8°$ BEVEL

2×6 P.T. SILL

DETAIL

$2\frac{1}{4}"$

$8°$

2×6 P.T.

$\frac{1}{8}"$ WIDE $\frac{1}{4}"$ DEEP DRIP GROOVE

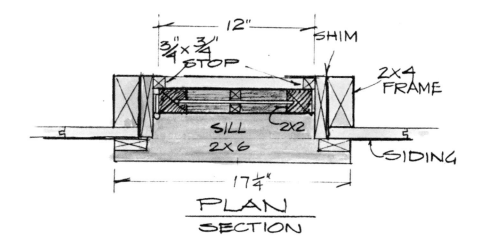

PLAN
SECTION

To join the window stiles and rails together at the corners, cut a 2" slot in the end of each 2×2, exactly in the center. Cut four 2"×2" right triangles out of ⅛" plywood. (This should be the width of your saw cut.) Trial-fit them into the corners.

Temporarily assemble the window sash. Measure and cut the muntin bars to fit in the grooves in the window sash. Mark and notch out where the muntins intersect. After checking that all the pieces fit, squeeze a bead of silicone into the grooves in the window sash, and set the glass into the silicone. Glue all the joints together using waterproof glue.

To make the window frame, cut a piece of 2×6 to a length of 17¼". Cut a 1¾"×4¼" notch at each end, leaving 1¼"×1¾" "ears" on the outside of the windowsill. Rip an 8-degree bevel along the top outside edge, and cut a ¼"-deep drip groove along the bottom outside.

Rip the 1×6 cedar to 4⁵⁄₁₆" wide, and cut two jambs to length (see detail at left). Cut the head jamb 13¾" long, and nail the frame together with 2½" galvanized finishing nails. Fit hinges to the sash, and hang the sash in the finished frame. Using the offcuts from ripping the jamb, cut window stops to length (about 24¼"), and nail them along the inside of the sash.

Siding

This garden house is sheathed in rough 1×6 tongue & groove cedar. (If you plan to paint it, use smooth tongue & groove cedar.) You will need approximately 37 pieces 6' long to cover the entire structure.

Starting at the right side of the door, cut 1" off the groove side of one board so that its edge is square, and face nail it along the doorframe, using 2" spiral- or ring-shank nails every 6". Nail a 2×4 parallel to and level with the base, to act as a temporary ledge on which to rest the boards. Slide each board onto the tongue of the preceding one and tap it in place, using a scrap piece of tongue and groove to protect the tongue of the board you are installing.

Toenail the boards to the top plate, the bottom frame, and the 2×4 nailer, using 2" siding nails. Toenailing the tongue & groove boards through the tongue will hide the nails (see detail at right). There is no need to nail the left side of the board (apart from the first one), since it is held by the tongue of the previous board. When you get to a corner, mark where the board extends past the post. Set your saw to 30 degrees, and rip two boards to fit together neatly at the corner. Continue around the garden house until you reach the other side of the door. Cut off the last board (to the left of the door) at right angles.

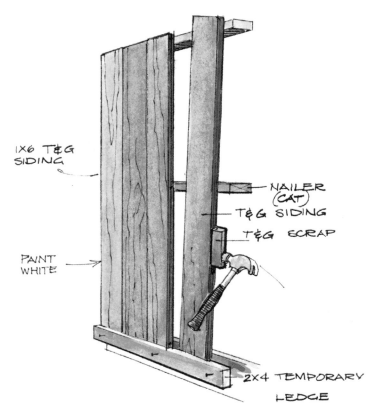

1×6 T&G SIDING

PAINT WHITE

NAILER (CAT)

T&G SIDING

T&G SCRAP

2×4 TEMPORARY LEDGE

SIDING NAIL

DETAIL

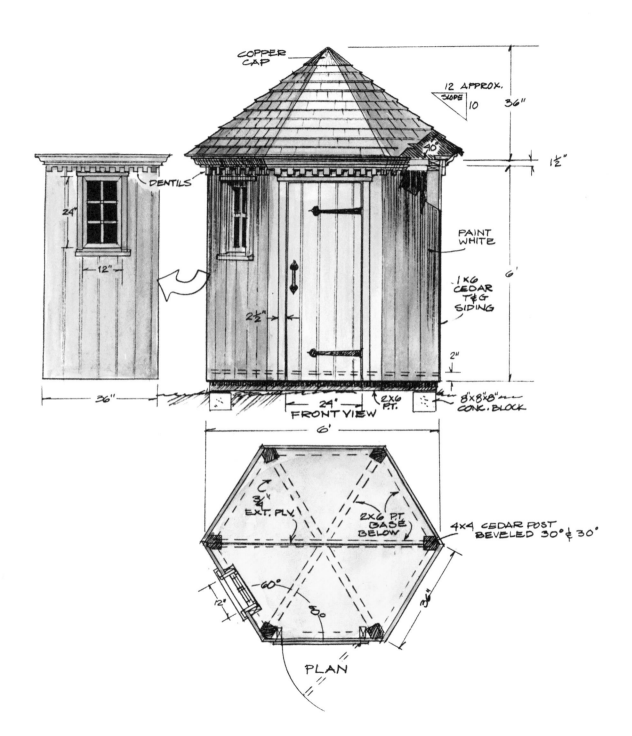

COPPER
CAP

12 APPROX.
SLOPE
10

36"

1½"

DENTILS

PAINT
WHITE

24"

6'

1×6
CEDAR
T&G
SIDING

12"

2½"

2"

36"

2×6
P.T.

24'

8"×8"×8"
CONC. BLOCK

FRONT VIEW

6'

¾"
EXT. PLY.

2×6 P.T.
BASE
BELOW

4×4 CEDAR POST
BEVELED 30° & 30°

60°

12"

60°

36"

PLAN

Dentils

From a clear piece of 1×2 cedar, cut 72 pieces 1¾" long, and 72 pieces 3½" long. Glue and nail them vertically to the front face of the cap plate, overlapping the top of the siding, so that they alternate in size (See page 113).

Cornice

To make the cornice, cut six pieces of 4½"-wide sprung crown molding into 48" lengths, which will allow you a few extra inches at each end for adjustments. Since the roof is six-sided, both ends of each strip of the cornice have to be cut at a compound angle. A simple miter jig will make these cuts much easier.

To construct the jig, use two 40"-long pieces of lumber, one 2×6 and the other 2×4. Measure 6" from each end of the 2×4 toward the center, and make a

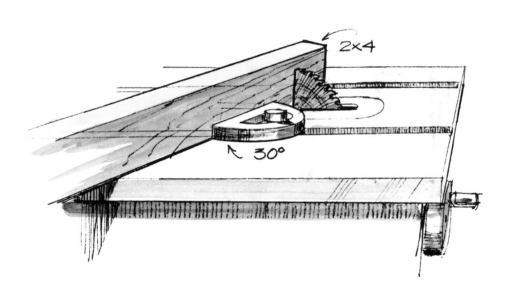

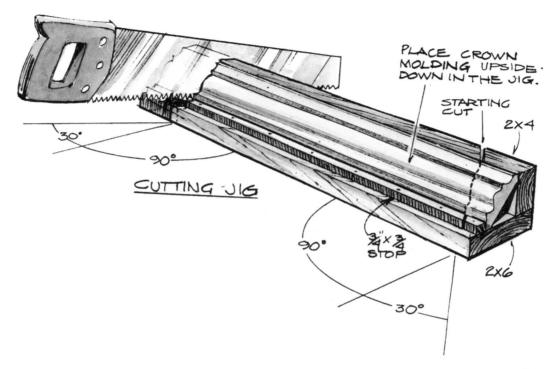

PLACE CROWN
MOLDING UPSIDE.
DOWN IN THE JIG.

STARTING
CUT

2×4

30°

90°

CUTTING JIG

90°

¾"×¾
STOP

30°

2×6

30-degree cut, sawing into the wood as far as the blade will allow. Screw the two pieces of wood together at right angles. Nail a 40"-long strip of ¾"×¾" wood to the 2×6 to hold the molding in place when cutting through it.

Before cutting the crown molding, measure the distance between each of the adjacent top corners of the shed. Turn the crown molding upside down in the jig, and place a hand saw in the guide cut of the jig to make a 30-degree compound cut at the end of each piece of cornice.

Most moldings are sprung at a 45-degree angle. Temporarily nail the crown molding onto a beveled 45-degree, 36"-long 1×6 (crown support), and rest it on the cap plate to test for fit. If necessary, make slight adjustments by sanding or filing the ends. Make a triangular support strip to fit between the crown molding and the crown support. This is a piece of lumber cut at a 45-degree bevel and glued to the back of the crown molding and the bottom front edge of the crown support. When all the pieces fit together perfectly, glue and screw the 1×6 crown support to the cap plate and to the outside of the dentils.

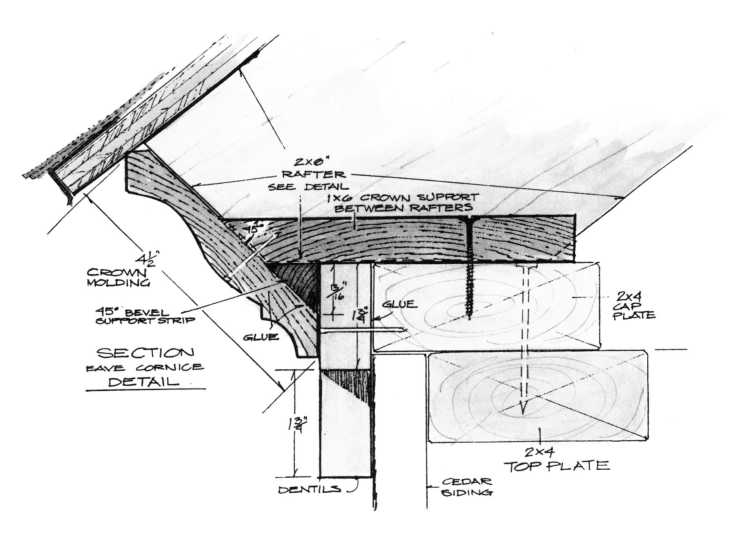

2x6" RAFTER
SEE DETAIL

1x6 CROWN SUPPORT
BETWEEN RAFTERS

15°

4½"
CROWN
MOLDING

45° BEVEL
SUPPORT STRIP

GLUE

SECTION
EAVE CORNICE
DETAIL

3/16"

1⅜"

GLUE

2x4
CAP
PLATE

2x4
TOP PLATE

1¾"

DENTILS

CEDAR
SIDING

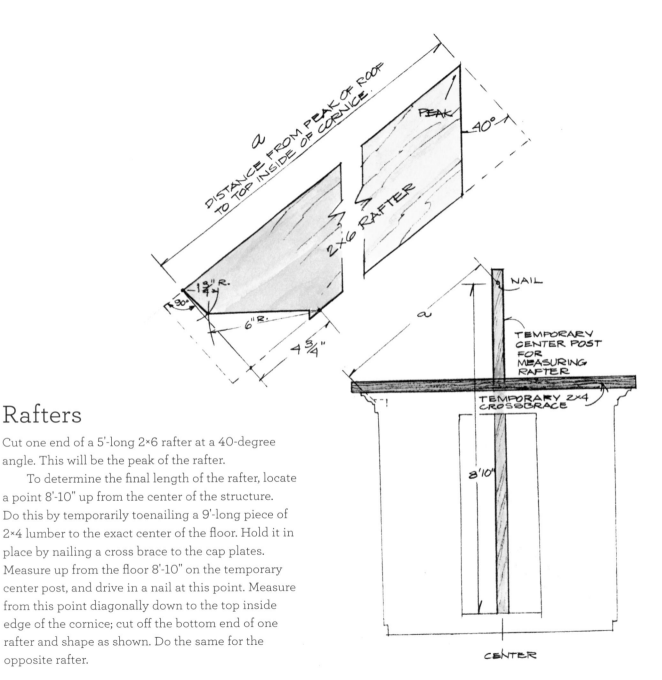

DISTANCE FROM PEAK OF ROOF TO TOP INSIDE OF CORNICE

a

2×6 RAFTER

PEAK

40°

1 9/4" R.

30°

6" R.

4 5/4"

NAIL

a

TEMPORARY CENTER POST FOR MEASURING RAFTER

TEMPORARY 2×4 CROSSBRACE

8'10"

CENTER

Rafters

Cut one end of a 5'-long 2×6 rafter at a 40-degree angle. This will be the peak of the rafter.

To determine the final length of the rafter, locate a point 8'-10" up from the center of the structure. Do this by temporarily toenailing a 9'-long piece of 2×4 lumber to the exact center of the floor. Hold it in place by nailing a cross brace to the cap plates. Measure up from the floor 8'-10" on the temporary center post, and drive in a nail at this point. Measure from this point diagonally down to the top inside edge of the cornice; cut off the bottom end of one rafter and shape as shown. Do the same for the opposite rafter.

Raise the first pair of rafters, temporarily nailing them together at the peak. Use the center pole to hold them in place. The remaining sets of rafters join the first pair at the peak. They will need to be slightly shorter than the first pair, with two beveled cuts at the peak end allowing them to fit together. Screw the rafters together with 3½" deck screws.

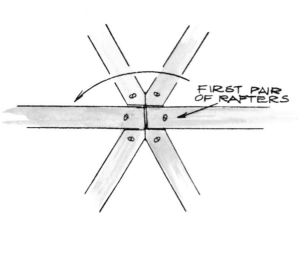

Roof

The roof is sheathed with ½" exterior plywood. Each panel will measure approximately 4'-10" along the long edges. Allow for a 1" overhang at the eaves. Check and adjust these dimensions. You will be able to cut two roof panels from one 4'×8' sheet of plywood. Use a chalk line to mark the cut lines. Set your saw blade at 10 degrees, and cut out the pieces. Nail the panels to the rafters using 2" nails, and cover the roof with #15 roofing felt and asphalt shingles.

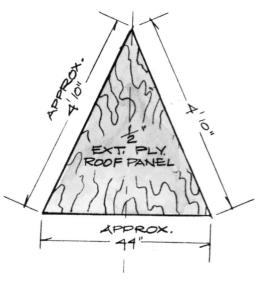

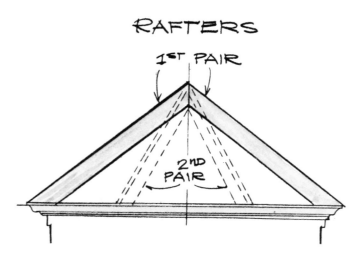

Door

Prepare the doorway by making a 29"-long head jamb out of ⁵⁄₄×6 P.T. lumber. Cut a notch out of each end so that the head jamb will fit inside the door opening, yet extend ¼" past the 2¼"-wide door trim on each side. Install the head jamb under the 2×4 top plate, using 2½" finishing nails.

To establish the height of the door, measure the distance from under the head jamb to the bottom of the siding. Cut five pieces of 1×6 tongue and groove cedar to this dimension. Lay the pieces face down on two sawhorses, and join them together temporarily. Mark and rip cut the two outside boards so that the door will measure 23¾", allowing for clearance (see front view, page 113). Cut two ⁵⁄₄×6 P.T. crosspieces

21½" long, and screw them to the back of the door using 1½" galvanized deck screws. For a perfect job, countersink the screws and bevel the edges of the battens.

Strengthen the door by running a ⁵⁄₄×4 diagonal brace from the top side opposite the hinge to the lower hinge side. Hang the door from two 18" black strap hinges, and fit a matching thumb latch.

To provide a surface for the door to rest against when it swings shut, cut two 6' pieces of 1×2 to act as a doorstop. Cut them to fit the sides of the door. Stand inside the garden house with the door closed and nail them in place, using 2½" galvanized finishing nails.

Cap

To top off this elegant garden structure, fit a copper cap over the peak of the roof. Find the center of a 24"-square sheet of 16oz. copper, and cut out a 24" circle. Mark and cut a straight line from one edge to the center of the copper, and bend it into a cone, overlapping the edges. Fit the cone to the peak of the roof and secure with 1½" copper nails.

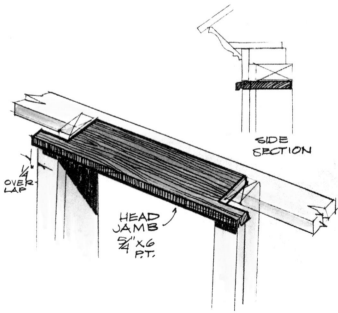

SIDE SECTION

¼" OVERLAP

HEAD JAMB ⁵⁄₄"×6 P.T.

Classic Cottage Garden Shed

Because of its simplicity, this classic cottage can be used as a potting shed, or be converted into an artist's studio or a children's playhouse. Other people have used this compact 7'×9' design for a writer's retreat, a yoga studio and even as extra accommodation for weekend guests. Keep it basic or wire it for electricity and plumbing—even add a skylight, depending on your preference. It's a practical design and size—one that can evolve as your needs change. It is especially attractive with a stain finish, or painted white or a dark Charleston green. Create a curving pebbled path leading up to the front door, and end it with a nice piece of slate or bluestone.

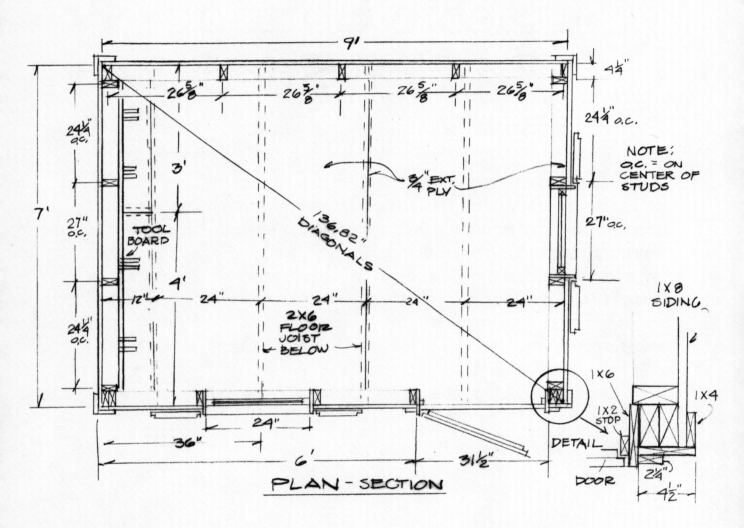

9'

4¼"

26 ⅝"   26 ⅝"   26 ⅝"   26 ⅝"

24¼" o.c.

24¼"
o.c.

3'

NOTE:
O.C. = ON
CENTER OF
STUDS

¾" EXT.
PLY

27"
o.c.

27" o.c.

7'

TOOL
BOARD

136.82"
DIAGONALS

4'

1X8
SIDING

12"   24"   24"   24"   24"

24¼"
o.c.

2X6
FLOOR
JOIST
BELOW

1X6

1X4

1'

1X2
STOP

DETAIL

24"

36"

6'

31½"

DOOR

2¼"

4½"

PLAN - SECTION

MATERIALS

BASE

2 10' 2×6 pressure-treated lumber *for base*

1 14' 2×6 pressure-treated lumber *for base*

2 14' 2×6 pressure-treated lumber *for floor joists*

4"×8"×16" solid concrete blocks *for base* (quantity varies)

Slate shims *for base* (quantity varies)

2 4'×8' ¾" exterior plywood *for floor*

WALLS

6 10' 2×4 construction fir *for front & back plates*

2 14' 2×4 construction fir *for end plates*

10 12' 2×4 construction fir *for horizontal nailers and window framing*

Note: fir & pine should be treated with clear preservative for outdoor use

384 linear feet 1×8 tongue & groove #2 pine *for siding*

ROOF

5 10' 2×4 #2 construction fir *for rafters*

1 4'×4' ½" plywood *for gusset plates*

1 10' 1×2 *for ridge pole*

1 roll 6"-wide insect screening *for eaves*

ROOF TRIM

2 10' 1×4 #2 pine *for fascia boards*

2 10' 1×4 #2 pine *for gable trim*

4 12' $^{11}\!/_{16}$"×1⅜" solid crown molding *for roof*

2 10' 1×6 *for eave boards*

22 10' 1×4 *for spaced sheathing*

ROOFING

5 bundles 18" premium red-cedar shingles *for roofing*

2 12' 1×4 #2 cedar *for ridge trim*

WINDOWS

2 8' 1×6 #2 pine *for window jambs*

2 10' 1×8 tongue & groove pine *for shutters*

1 8' 1×4 #2 pine *for shutter batten*

DOOR

1 12' 1×8 tongue & groove #2 pine *for door*

2 12' 1×6 #2 pine *for door battens & jamb*

2 10' ¼"×1⅛" lattice *for insect screen*

5 12' 1×4 #2 pine *for door trim, diagonal door brace, and corner boards*

3 18" wrought-iron strap hinges

4 lbs. 3½" common nails

4 lbs. 2" spiral- or ring-shank siding nails

1 lb. 1¼" galvanized deck screws

SHELF

1 12' 1×12 #2 pine *for shelf*

1 12' 1×2 #2 pine *for shelf front trim*

1 8' 1×6 *for tool board*

1 3' 1"-diameter wooden dowel *for tool pegs*

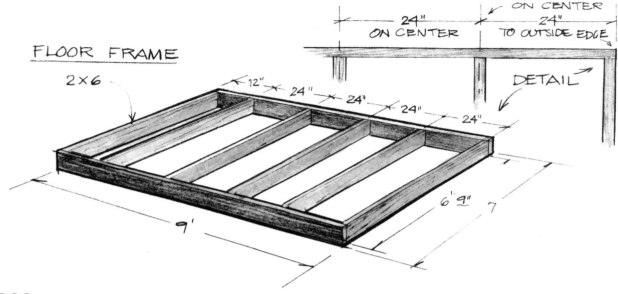

FLOOR FRAME

2×6

12" · 24" · 24" · 24" · 24"

9'

6'-9" · 7

24" ON CENTER · ON CENTER 24" TO OUTSIDE EDGE

DETAIL

Base

Begin by building a level base. Cut two pieces of 2×6 lumber to 9', and two more to 6'-9". Nail them together into a 7'×9' rectangle, using 3½" common nails. Cut four 2×6 P.T. floor joists 6'-9" long, and nail them inside and at right angles to the long sides, spaced 24" on centers. Place the last floor joist 12" from the end. Measurements are made from outside of frame to center of joist.

Adjust for any unevenness in your building site by shoring up the base. Do this by laying the frame on concrete blocks at the low end of your building site. Use solid concrete blocks (4"×8"×16") stacked as necessary. If you need more than three blocks together, consider switching to 12"-diameter cardboard Sonotubes: these are buried 36" deep in the ground,

and filled with concrete to form piers. Add slate shims between the blocks and the frame to make it perfectly level. For several days, periodically check that the frame has not settled out of level.

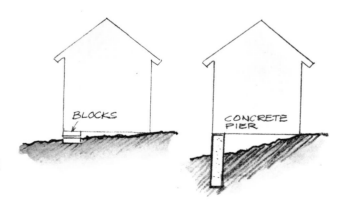

BLOCKS

CONCRETE PIER

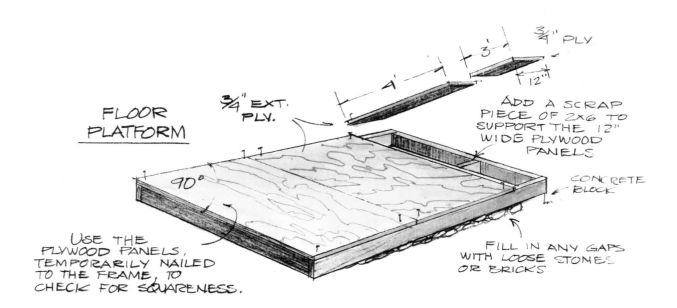

FLOOR PLATFORM

¾" EXT. PLY.

90°

USE THE PLYWOOD PANELS, TEMPORARILY NAILED TO THE FRAME, TO CHECK FOR SQUARENESS.

4'

3'

¾" PLY

12"

ADD A SCRAP PIECE OF 2x6 TO SUPPORT THE 12" WIDE PLYWOOD PANELS

CONCRETE BLOCK

FILL IN ANY GAPS WITH LOOSE STONES OR BRICKS

Floor

Cut two pieces of ¾" exterior plywood to 4'×7', and nail them on top of the floor frame. Temporarily nail all four corners of each piece of plywood to the frame, to make sure the frame is square. Double-check by measuring the diagonals: they should be 136⅞", and identical. Nail the plywood to the frame with 2" siding nails at 6" intervals. Use the leftover plywood to cover the 12"-wide opening at one end of the floor.

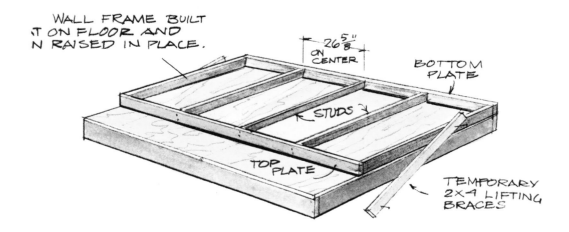

Walls

Build the back wall first, by cutting two 2×4s into 9' plates, and five 2×4s into 69" studs. Using the floor as a work platform, nail the 2×4 top and bottom plates to the ends of the studs, 26⅝" on centers.

Lift up the back wall frame and secure it in place with two 2×4 braces, nailed to the sides of the wall and to the sides of the floor frame.

Build the two end walls in the same way. Cut 77"-long top and bottom plates, to allow for the thickness of the front and rear walls. Cut four 69"-long studs for each end wall. Once they are assembled, stand them up and temporarily nail them to the back wall frame.

Build the front wall to the dimensions shown in the plan, doubling the number of corner studs for extra strength. After checking that the measurements are correct and the frame is square and plumb (vertical), nail the 2×4s together permanently with 3½" common nails.

To make sure the frame stays in alignment while you are completing the structure, temporarily nail 1×4 diagonal braces to the inside walls. Complete the frame by cutting and nailing a second layer of 2×4s (cap plate) over the top plates.

To strengthen the walls, toenail 2×4 nailers horizontally between the studs, 33¾" up from the floor. Cut two pieces of 2×4, 25½" long, and nail them between the studs at each of the two window locations.

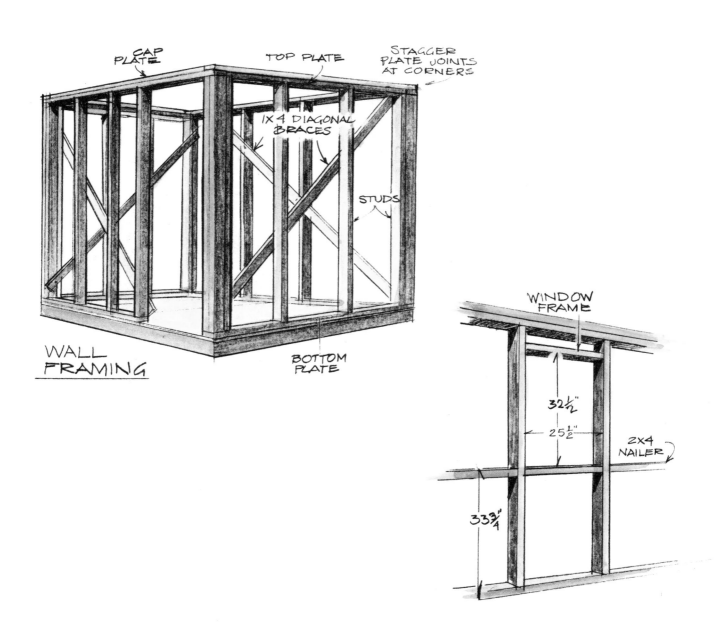

CAP PLATE

TOP PLATE

STAGGER PLATE JOINTS AT CORNERS

1 X 4 DIAGONAL BRACES

STUDS

WALL FRAMING

BOTTOM PLATE

WINDOW FRAME

$32\frac{1}{2}"$

$25\frac{1}{2}"$

2X4 NAILER

$33\frac{3}{4}"$

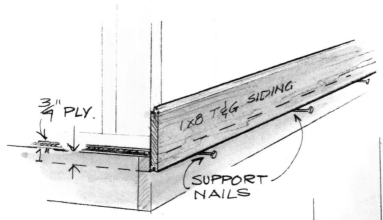

Siding

To cover the walls with horizontal sheathing, you will need approximately 384 linear feet of 1×8 tongue & groove #2 pine. Partially hammer three nails into the 2×6 base of each side, 1" below the ¾" plywood floor. Use these as a ledge on which to rest the first course of sheathing. Start at the back and work around, one course at a time, using 2" spiral- or ring-shank siding nails.

Face nail the first row of boards at the bottom, and toenail them at the top. The remaining boards are held at the bottom by the tongue & groove, and toenailed into the tongue at the top of each successive board. Continue until you reach the top, rip cutting the last course if necessary so that the board fits below the cap plate.

Rafters

The five pairs of 2×4 rafters are joined at the peaks by ½" plywood gusset plates. Begin by cutting a 10'-long 2×4 in half. Cut a 54-degree angle on one end of each piece. Using an electric jig saw, cut a bird's mouth notch to allow the rafters to sit on the top plate.

Join the rafters at the top with 24"-wide triangular gusset plates, cut from a piece of ½" plywood. Make the gussets by cutting an 8½"-wide by 24"-long rectangle, and cut off the two sides at 36.5-degree angles. Nail the gusset plates to the rafters, using 2" siding nails.

Cut a ¾"×1½" notch out of the center peaks to accept a 1×2 ridgepole. Mark the ridgepole at 26⅝" intervals. With an assistant, set up the two outside pairs of rafters (trusses) first, then the three inner pairs. Rest the 10'-long ridgepole in the notches.

Staple a 6"-wide piece of aluminum insect screening to the top edge of the front and rear siding and to the bottoms of the rafters.

Finish nailing the siding on both gable ends. Let the ends of the siding overhang the tops of the rafters, then snap a chalk line and cut them off in one pass, using an electric circular saw. If any of the siding boards protrude above the rafters, this will create a bump in the roof.

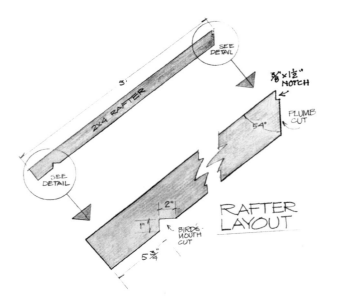

RAFTER LAYOUT

Finishing the Roof

Nail a 10'-long 1×4 fascia to the ends of the rafters using 2" siding nails, allowing 6" to extend beyond each end wall. Nail a 10'-long 1×6 over the rafters and the fascia. Cut four 1×4s 5' long for the gable trim; cut off one end of each at a 54-degree angle to fit together at the top. Notch out the top of the gable trim to accept the end of the 1×2 ridgepole.

To support the cedar shingles, attach two 10'-long 1×4 nailers above each of the 1×6s along the eaves. Allow a 2" space and add another nailer, continuing up the roof until you reach the peak. Fix the ends of the nailers to the gable trim.

Finish off the roof framing by adding ¹¹⁄₁₆"×1⅜"

solid crown molding to the eaves and the gables. For a professional, finished appearance, miter the corner moldings where they meet.

Use five bundles of red cedar shingles to cover the roof. Double the first course, and overlap the gables and eave edge by ½". Nail on each course 5½" above the preceding one, making sure to stagger the shingles so the joints don't line up. Use a chalk line or a straight piece of 1×4 to keep the lines straight.

Cover the peak with two 121"-long pieces of cedar. Rip cut each at a 54-degree bevel along one edge before they are nailed together.

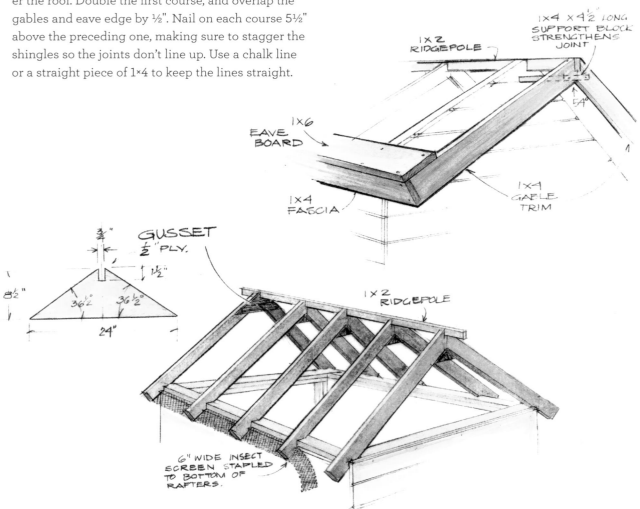

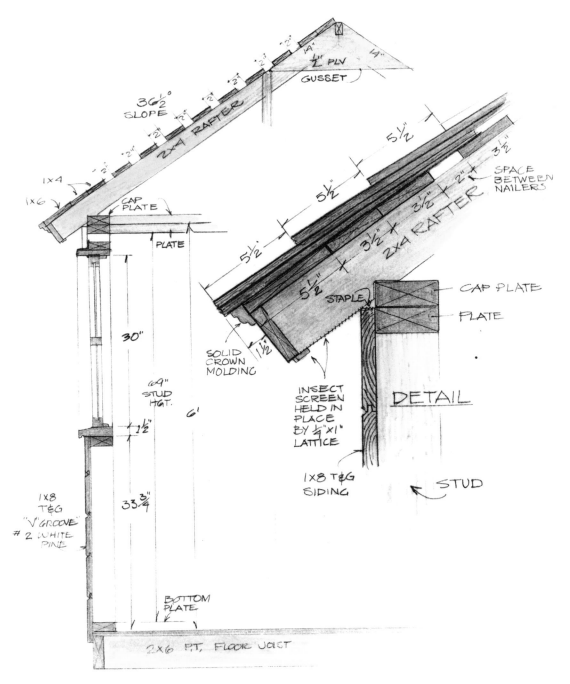

$36\frac{1}{2}°$ SLOPE

2"

2"

2"

2"

2"

2"

2"

2"

2"

2×4 RAFTER

$\frac{1}{2}"$ PLУ

GUSSET

4"

1×4

1×6

CAP PLATE

PLATE

$5\frac{1}{2}$

$3\frac{1}{2}$

2×4 RAFTER

2"

$3\frac{1}{2}$

SPACE BETWEEN NAILERS

$5\frac{1}{2}$

$3\frac{1}{2}$

$5\frac{1}{2}$

$5\frac{1}{2}$

$5\frac{1}{2}$

STAPLE

CAP PLATE

PLATE

30"

69" STUD HGT.

6'

$1\frac{1}{2}$

$1\frac{1}{2}$

SOLID CROWN MOLDING

INSECT SCREEN HELD IN PLACE BY $\frac{1}{4}"×1"$ LATTICE

DETAIL

1×8 T&G SIDING

STUD

$33\frac{3}{4}"$

1×8 T&G "V" GROOVE #2 WHITE PINE

BOTTOM PLATE

2×6 P.T. FLOOR JOIST

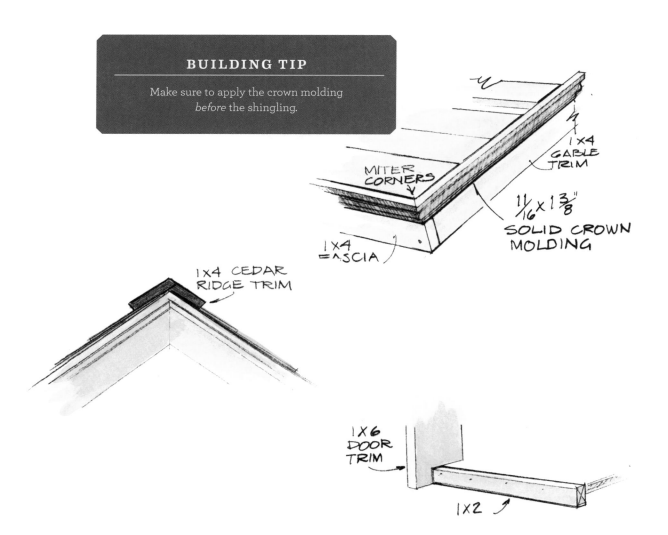

BUILDING TIP

Make sure to apply the crown molding *before* the shingling.

1X4 GABLE TRIM

MITER CORNERS

$\frac{11}{16} \times 1\frac{3}{8}$" SOLID CROWN MOLDING

1X4 FASCIA

1X4 CEDAR RIDGE TRIM

1X6 DOOR TRIM

1X2

Finishing Touches

The shutters on this cottage can be decorative or functional. Whether they are left natural, stained, or painted, they give the building a more finished appearance.

To build shutters for two windows, cut eight pieces of 1×8 tongue & groove 24" long. Cut 1" off the grooves of four pieces and 1" off the tongues of the others, so that the total width of each shutter panel is 12". To make the horizontal battens, cut eight pieces of 1×4, 10" long, and position one 3" from the bottom and one 3" from the top of each shutter. Screw the battens to the shutters with 1¼" galvanized deck screws. For a more professional job, counterbore and fill the holes with wooden plugs. Hinge or screw the shutters to the window.

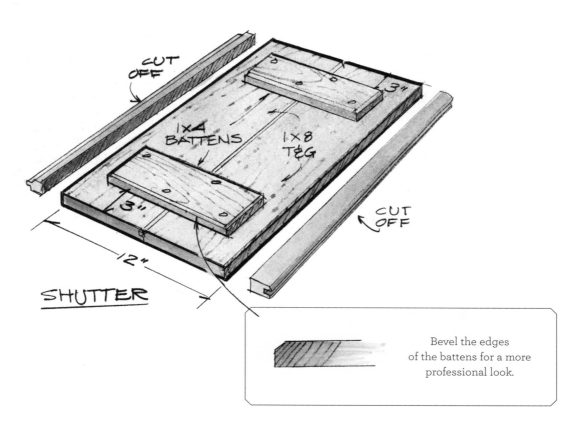

CUT OFF

1×4 BATTENS

1×8 T&G

3"

3"

12"

SHUTTER

CUT OFF

Bevel the edges of the battens for a more professional look.

Summerhouse

More than a summerhouse, this structure can be enjoyed all year round. Even in the winter it gets lots of warmth and light from the sun beaming through the slatted roof, while the combination doors keep it snug and draft-free; and as the hot weather approaches, simply install the screen doors for cross-ventilation. The summerhouse is perfect for the corner of a garden, perhaps coming into view after a turn in a path.

The design is an octagon composed of combination screen and storm doors. The lath boards in the roof allow sunlight to filter through without glare. It is an ideal place to read, write, or enjoy a few moments of solitude after a morning of gardening. We built the summerhouse for a couple who like to play chess in the winter and paint watercolors in the summer, with a view of the bay and passing swan. If possible, run an underground electric line to the summerhouse, so it can sparkle with lights in the evening—like a jewel box. For the ultimate effect, dig a shallow moat in which the building will be reflected—two for the price of one.

MATERIALS

OCTAGONAL DECK

8 8' 4×4 pressure-treated lumber *for deck posts*

7 6' 4×4 pressure-treated lumber *for deck outer posts & center post*

8 12' 2×6 pressure-treated lumber *for deck joists*

4 12' 2×8 pressure-treated lumber *for floor joists*

35 10' 2×6 pressure-treated lumber *for deck & floor*

SUMMERHOUSE

8 7' 4×4 cedar posts *for wall corners*

8 10' 2×4 #2 fir *for top plates*

32 7' 2×4 #2 fir *for door (rough framing)*

8 7' 2×6 #2 fir *for rafters*

Note: fir & pine should be treated with clear preservative for outdoor use

4 4'×8' ¼" clear Plexiglas *for skylight*

8 7' 2×2 cedar planks *for skylight (triangular strips)*

8 7' 2×2 aluminum edge flashing *for skylight*

1 18" 4×4 clear cedar *for roof (center post)*

1 4'×4' ½" exterior plywood *for roof cap*

1 9' 24" copper flashing *for roof cap*

16 7' 1×6 #2 pine *for doorjambs*

16 38" 1×6 #2 pine *for door headers*

16 7' 1×8 #2 pine *for exterior trim*

16 7' 1×6 #2 pine *for interior trim*

16 7' 1×4 #2 pine *for exterior trim*

8 7' 1×3 #2 pine *for interior block*

32 7' ½"×1⅝" casing *for trim*

3 4'×8' ½" exterior plywood *for soffits*

3 4'×8' ¾" exterior plywood *for roof extension*

8 3'×6'-8" combination storm/screen French doors

1 Lock set, entry type with key *for front door*

4 1⅛"×3" brass hinges *for doors*

8 decorative wall brackets *for doors*

240 linear ft. 1×4 #2 pine *for roof slats*

1 35' ³⁄₁₆" stainless-steel cable *for rafters*

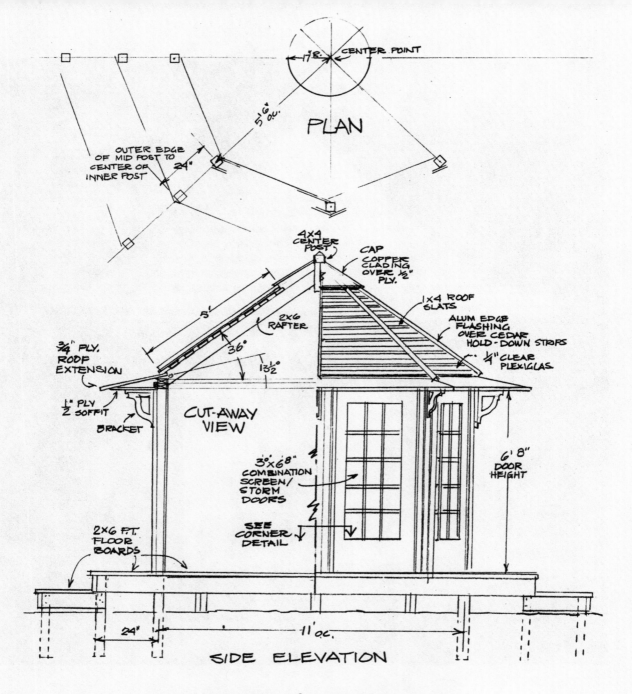

PLAN

CENTER POINT

18"

5'-6" O.C.

OUTER EDGE OF MID POST TO CENTER OR INNER POST

24"

4×4 CENTER POST

CAP COPPER CLADING OVER ½" PLY.

1×4 ROOF SLATS

ALUM EDGE FLASHING OVER CEDAR HOLD-DOWN STRIPS

¼" CLEAR PLEXIGLAS

5'

2×6 RAFTER

36°

13½°

¾" PLY. ROOF EXTENSION

½" PLY. SOFFIT

BRACKET

CUT-AWAY VIEW

3°×6'8" COMBINATION SCREEN/ STORM DOORS

SEE CORNER DETAIL

6'8" DOOR HEIGHT

2×6 P.T. FLOOR BOARDS

24"

11' O.C.

SIDE ELEVATION

Layout

This summerhouse looks best surrounded by an octagonal deck: although not essential, this gives the effect of a pedestal, and creates a gradual transition from the ground to the structure.

Clear an area 24' in diameter and establish a center point for a 19'-diameter circle, driving a stake into the ground.

Make a compass out of a 10'-long board by driving a heavy nail into one end and nailing a pointed stick to the other end. Use the stick to scribe two circles on the ground—one with a 9'-6" radius and another with a 5'-6" radius. Scribe a line through the centers of the circles, and another at right angles to it. Bisect the four resultant quadrants, creating eight equidistant points around the circumference of both circles. Mark all the points with wooden pegs.

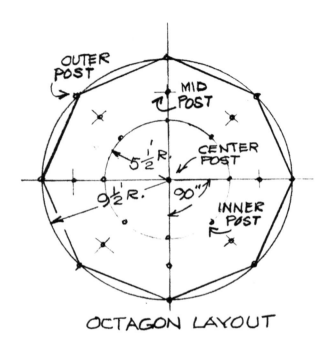

OCTAGON LAYOUT

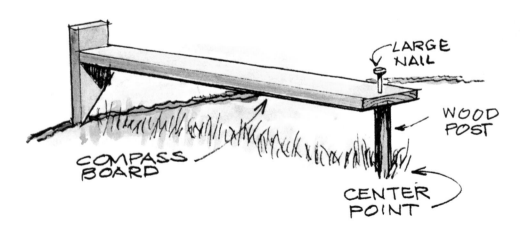

Floor Framing

Dig 30"-deep holes directly over the inner circle points, and bury the ends of the 48"-long 4×4 posts in the ground. Don't backfill until you are sure they are perfectly aligned. Dig another set of holes 2' out from the first set, and bury eight 48"-long middle posts in the ground. Dig a third set of holes 2' out from these, and bury eight more 4×4s in the ground (to support the deck). Connect the middle and outer posts with a 2×6 joist screwed to each side of each post.

To provide support for the floor of the summer-house, make an octagonal center post by using a table saw to cut 1½" off each corner of a 4×4 post, at a 45-degree angle. Bury this center support post so that the top is level with the inner and middle posts. Nail the 2×8 joists radially from the center post to the inner posts, toenailing to the center post and using joist hangers for the inner posts.

Cut 2×6 pressure-treated floorboards at 67.5-degree angles at the ends, and nail them to the 2×8 floor joists in concentric hexagons.

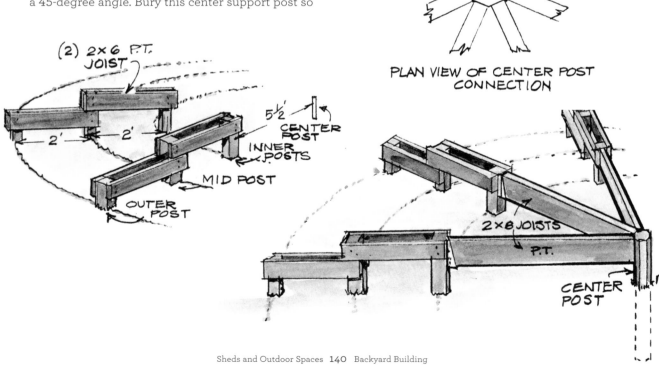

PLAN VIEW OF CENTER POST
CONNECTION

Wall Framing

To frame the summerhouse, begin by erecting eight 4×4 corner posts 6'-9" long. Connect the posts with two layers of 2×4 top plates attached as shown. Find and mark the center between each pair of posts, and mark 19" either side of this. The space between these marks allows for the 36"-wide doors, ¾" for each door jamb, and ¼" to shim each jamb. Screw a 2×4 stud to the floor and to the top plates at the outside of the marks. To make the door frames (jambs), rip ½" off the 1×6 boards so that the boards are 5" wide, and use them to build eight U-shaped (upside down) door frames.

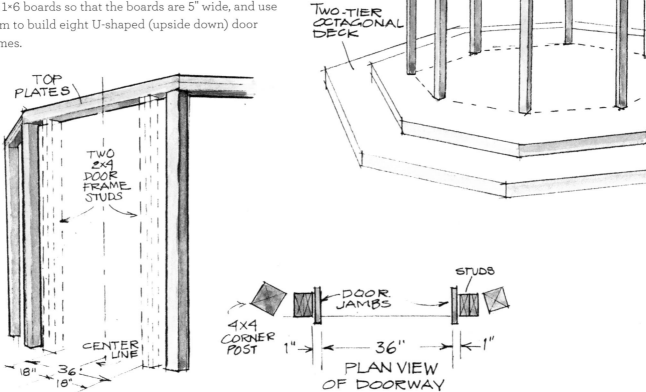

2×4

PLAN VIEW

DOUBLE 2×4 TOP PLATES

TWO-TIER OCTAGONAL DECK

TOP PLATES

TWO 2×4 DOOR FRAME STUDS

CENTER LINE

18"   36"   18"

4×4 CORNER POST

DOOR JAMBS

STUDS

1"   36"   1"

PLAN VIEW OF DOORWAY

Pre-cut door frames (jambs and headers) are often sold at lumberyards. Place the door frames in the doorways. Using one of the doors as a spacer, shim and screw the door frames to the studs. Allow a ³⁄₁₆" gap on all sides of the door to allow for expansion of the wood. Cut and nail a ³⁄₈"×1³⁄₈" doorstop for the door to rest against when it is closed.

Rafters

To temporarily support the rafters at the top, install an 11'-5" 4×4 post in the exact center of the summerhouse. Before setting up the post, cut 45 degrees off each corner to make eight equal faces on the top end of the post where the rafters will meet. To make the rafters, cut 8 2×6s 7' long. Cut a 54-degree angle at the top and a notch at the bottom of each rafter.

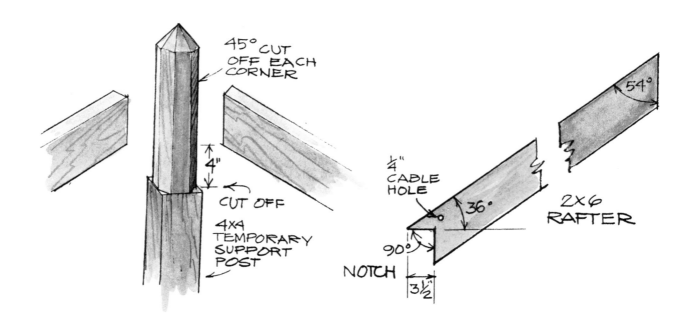

Slats

To allow the sun to filter through the roof, fix 1×4s horizontally, spaced 3½" apart (see Side Elevation—page 138). (Use a piece of 1×4 as a spacer.) If you plan to paint the summerhouse, make sure that you paint both sides of the 1×4s first.

Optional

Before installing the rafters, cut a chase (slot) in the bottom of one to provide space for an electric cable. The cut can be disguised by inserting a removable strip of wood trimmed to fit.

Install a rafter at each corner, using two ¼"×4½" lag screws at right angles to each other.

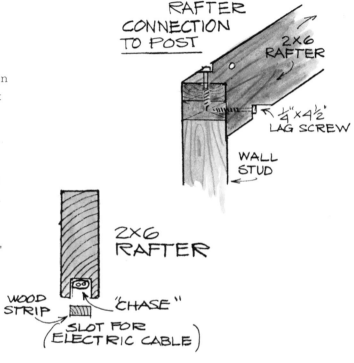

Compression Cable

To keep the rafters from spreading under the weight of the roof, run a ³⁄₁₆"-diameter stainless-steel cable through ¼" holes drilled near the base of each. Make a loop at each end of the cable, and connect the two ends with a turnbuckle and cable clamps (or a swaging sleeve). Tighten the cable by turning the turnbuckle. When the cable is taut, cut off the center post 4" below the bottom edge of the rafter heads.

Skylight

To keep out the rain, install a Plexiglas roof on top of the slats. Two sections can be cut from a ¼"-thick 4'×8' sheet of Plexiglas with minimum waste. If you're having it cut for you, cut a piece of ¼" plywood to size, test fit it on all sides of the skylight to check that the dimensions haven't changed, and take it to the glass store as a template.

Plexiglas tends to expand and contract with changes in temperature; you must therefore (slowly!) drill oversize (¼") screw holes to allow it some movement. In addition, the adjoining pieces should not butt together but be spaced ½" apart. Fill the gap with clear Silicone sealant, held in place with a triangular piece of cedar, ripped to fit the angle where the two pieces of Plexiglas meet. Screw the cedar strips to the top edge of the rafters, using 3" stainless-steel screws.

To protect the cedar strips from weathering, cover them with 2"×2" aluminum edge flashing, which is sold in most lumberyards. Paint the flashing before you install it, and hold the pieces in place with construction adhesive.

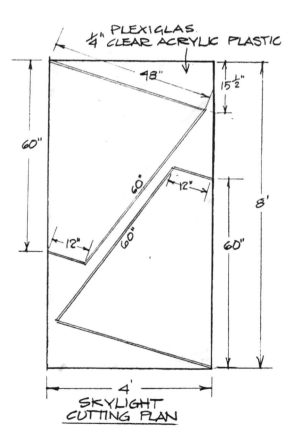

¼" PLEXIGLAS
¼" CLEAR ACRYLIC PLASTIC

48"

15½"

60"

60"

12"

12"

60"

8'

60"

4'

SKYLIGHT CUTTING PLAN

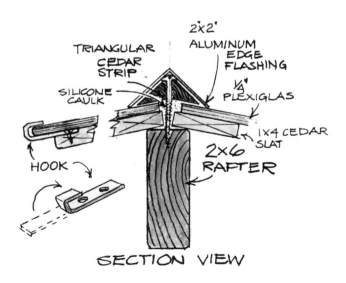

TRIANGULAR CEDAR STRIP

2"×2" ALUMINUM EDGE FLASHING

SILICONE CAULK

¼" PLEXIGLAS

1×4 CEDAR SLAT

2×6 RAFTER

HOOK

SECTION VIEW

Cap

Make the octagonal cap out of ½"-thick plywood, joined together by galvanized metal straps and fitted into a ½" slot in the top center post. The plywood lies on top of the triangular cedar strips and allows a 2" space for ventilation. This space can be screened in if bugs are a problem. Cover the cap with copper bent over the plywood and joined at the seams. Over time, this will weather to an aqua green. While you're working at the peak, bore a ½"-diameter hole 9" deep in the top of the center post, to hold a weathervane.

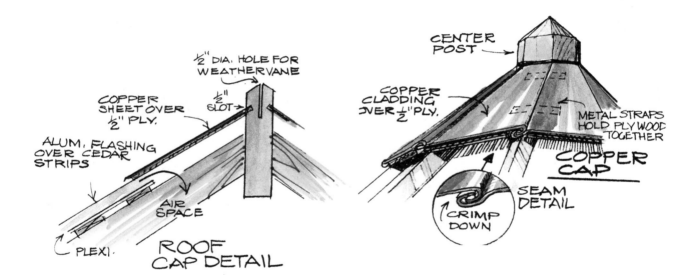

Wall Corner Trim

Cut and nail 1×8s to the outside corners and 1×6s to the inside corners. Add ½"×1⅝" trim (casing) to the interior and exterior of each doorway, and 1×4s to the outside corners. Add a filler block between the two 1×6s on the inside corners.

Roof Extension

Cut 8 pieces of ¾" plywood 30" deep to fit under the bottom edge of the Plexiglas. They should be deep enough that rainwater will not seep back inside the summerhouse.

To support the plywood roof extensions, buy or build wall brackets and attach them to the corner trim boards. Build a ½" ply soffit over the tops of the brackets to support the outside of the roof extensions.

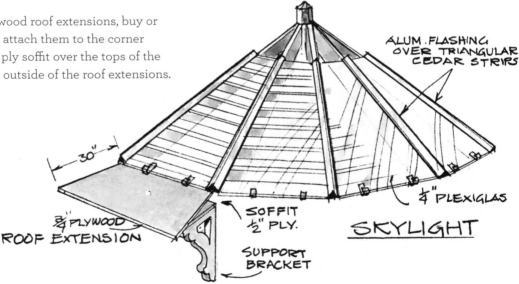

Doors

It's easier to paint the doors before you install them. Attach hinges and handles to the doors that will be operable; seal the rest with caulking adhesive.

3

Treehouses and Playhouses

A treehouse is unique—literally so, since trees are as individual as people (and come in even more shapes, sizes and colors). Part of our business is designing treehouses for specific sites, but here we give general advice on how to build using one or more trees for support—or even no tree at all. The structure doesn't have to be high, either: it's just something about being off the ground that makes it exciting and different.

PLANNING A TREEHOUSE

All children want a space of their own, and left to their own devices will make one under a dining table, from a cardboard box, or using a blanket and a chair. Building a backyard playhouse is as easy as building a shed—but try to add child-friendly features such as windows, a loft with a ladder, etc., to engage their imagination; and (with apologies to over-sized parents) make it to fit them, not you: it's their place after all.

Sometimes it's difficult to visualize just how the treehouse will fit into the tree. One way to do this is to get several lengths of wood (rough 1×2s will do), climb into the tree and make a temporary frame held together with screws—or even duct tape. You'll get a better idea of how your treehouse will look, and can take accurate measurements once you're happy with the layout.

We are always interested to see the different inventive ways people meet the challenges: for example, Jon Mulder supported his treehouse on braces alone, and the tree grows right through the middle.

We cradled the Hobbit Treehouse (at left) among several strong curving branches; the Thatched Treehouse rests against the tree and is supported by sturdy posts at the front. This illustrates the way that the tree itself influences the design.

The following two treehouses are each built using one tree and two posts, but the results are very different. The Peace Treehouse is open on two sides and only partially enclosed on the others, whereas the Hollywood Treehouse is completely enclosed, shingled on three sides, and fitted with windows. The Peace Treehouse has a traditional ridged roof, while the Hollywood Treehouse has a more elaborate four-sided thatched roof with a cupola. Because of its three-sided deck, the Hollywood Treehouse has posts with knee-braces to make it extra secure. The Peace Treehouse has a ladder integrated into the tree, while the Hollywood Treehouse ladder is more like a stairway.

There's more than one way to build a treehouse in a single tree. If your tree isn't big enough or the right shape to enclose a house, you can supplement the tree trunk using other supports: either braces attached to the tree trunk, or posts that allow you to build a more substantial overhanging deck.

RIDGE POLE & PULLEY

SCALLOPED SHINGLES

24" SHAKES

1x4 NAILERS

ROOF SUPPORT POST

1x6 CEDAR T&G

5/8" ROPE

2x6 RAFTERS

4x4 DECK POST

HOLE FOR BRANCH

5/4 x 6 DECKING

MAIN 2x8 FLOOR BEAMS

ENTRANCE LADDER

2x8 FLOOR JOISTS

2x6

6" Ø CEDAR LOG DEBARKED

CONCRETE FOOTING

Peace Treehouse

Every tree is different, and so is every treehouse. This design was tailor-made for its situation, but the principles are the same for any playhouse built in a single tree, and can be applied and elaborated to suit your own circumstances and needs.

Our client wanted his two girls to have a real treehouse, but not too high off the ground. The first sketch had a picket-style railing, which we later changed to our "signature" style rope railing finials. The roof suggests the form of a bird's wing, with a graceful curve and shingles layered like feathers. The peace symbol was especially requested by one of the girls.

Working from photos supplied by our client, we were intending to attach the stairs to the front deck, but once at the site we immediately saw a natural opening between the two main trunks of the tree—perfect for a child to pass through. This, along with a child-sized gate at the opening, made access to the treehouse much more interesting. It really engages kids' imagination and creativity if you can enrich their play-space with lots of little features like this. The curved rafter tails are made by gluing and screwing 2×4s to 2×6s, and cutting the profiles with a jigsaw.

MATERIALS

2	12'	2×8 pressure-treated lumber *for main girders*
2	4'	4×4 construction cedar *for deck corner posts*
2	6'	2×8 construction cedar *for crossbeams*
2	8'	6"-diameter cedar trees, debarked *for support posts*
7	14'	⁵⁄₄×6 pressure-treated lumber *for deck*
3	8'	2×8 pressure-treated lumber *for floor joists*
4	8'	4×4 construction cedar *for roof support posts*
56'		1×6 tongue & groove clear cedar *for sides & front gable*
40'		1×6 tongue & groove clear cedar *for back wall*
4	10'	2×4 construction cedar *for railing*
8	6'	2×6 pressure-treated lumber *for rafters*
2	10'	2×4 pressure-treated lumber *for rafter tails*
2	8'	2×8 pressure-treated lumber *for crossbeams*
12	10'	1×4 #2 pine *for roof nailers*

Note: pine should be treated with clear preservative for outdoor use

2		Cedar post caps *for railing posts*
2	8'	2×6 pressure-treated lumber *for rear entrance*
4 bundles		24" hand-split shingles (shakes) *for roof*
2	10'	2×6 pressure-treated lumber *for ladder*
1	12'	2×4 pressure-treated lumber *for ladder steps*
6		³⁄₈"×4" galvanized carriage bolts with nuts & washers
1 box		1¾" galvanized nails
2 boxes		6d galvanized common nails
1 box		2½" deck screws
4		½"×5" lag screws
2		80lb. bags concrete mix
140'		⁵⁄₈" Hempex rope *for deck railing*

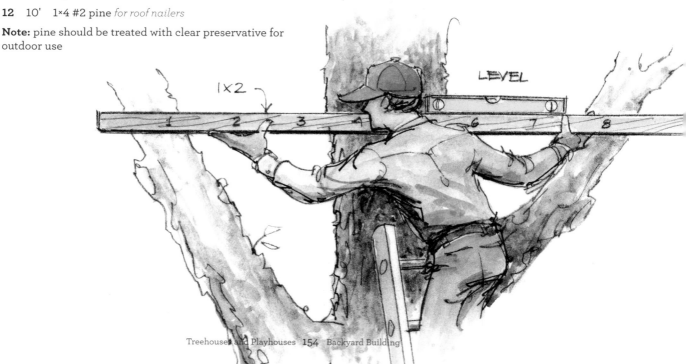

The first job is always to establish a level platform for the floor. Deciding where to attach the floor beams is perhaps the most difficult part of the building. You also need to be sure that the tree can accommodate the height of the treehouse. Take into consideration the age and height of your kids and how long they will continue to be treehouse dwellers. A measuring stick (made from a 12' 1×2 marked every foot with clearly legible numbers) will help you to determine how your treehouse can best fit in the tree, and to figure out the length of the main beams.

It's usually better to keep the floor about six or seven feet from the ground: it's easier and safer to build the platform of a treehouse from the ground;

the supporting tree will be much stronger at this height than at the crown, and less likely to be affected by the wind; and treehouses are less conspicuous closer to the ground, and a bit easier for young children to navigate.

You may find that you have to saw off a few branches to make room. This will not harm the tree, and in many cases a little pruning is beneficial. You could also let some of the tree limbs stick through the roof: it's a bit more work, but seems somehow more respectful of the host tree—and it certainly adds interest to the treehouse.

Supports for the treehouse are another consideration. Posts are the easiest, and allow usable space underneath the tree to sit, walk or play. On the other hand, braces blend in more with the tree trunk and are less noticeable. You can even make braces from branches sawn off the tree itself, disguising the fact that you needed braces at all.

The ideal treehouse is one that looks as if it had grown out of the tree. The Hobbit Treehouse (above) has cedar shingles arranged more like a natural pine-cone than a man-made roof.

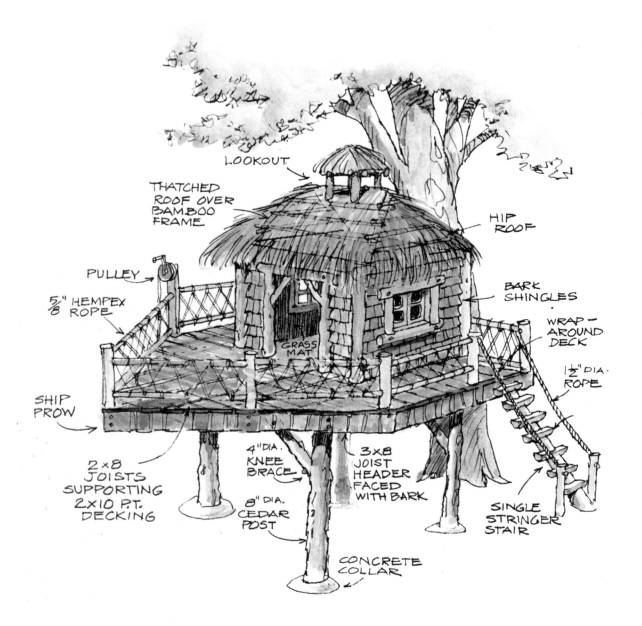

LOOKOUT

THATCHED
ROOF OVER
BAMBOO
FRAME

HIP
ROOF

PULLEY

$\frac{5}{8}$" HEMPEX
ROPE

BARK
SHINGLES

WRAP-
AROUND
DECK

SHIP
PROW

GRASS
MAT

$1\frac{1}{2}$" DIA.
ROPE

2×8
JOISTS
SUPPORTING
2×10 P.T.
DECKING

4" DIA.
KNEE
BRACE

3×8
JOIST
HEADER
FACED
WITH BARK

SINGLE
STRINGER
STAIR

8" DIA.
CEDAR
POST

CONCRETE
COLLAR

Hollywood Treehouse

Like any form of architecture, a treehouse should have a style of its own to reflect the owners' tastes and interests. We always suggest that our clients sit down as a family to discuss the appearance and specific features they'd like: some may want the treehouse to look woodsy, and be made of logs and branches, while others are thinking of a pirate ship, a stockade fort, or even a fairytale castle.

MATERIALS

Note: This materials list is for our specific tree and site, and should be adjusted for your own situation.

4	12'	8"-diameter Cedar logs *for posts*
1	12'	10"-diameter Cedar logs *for stairs*
2	6'	4"-diameter Cedar logs *for braces*
13	8'	5"-diameter (peeled) Cedar logs *for rail posts*
6	10'	5"-diameter (peeled) Cedar logs *for newel posts and braces*
1	10'	3"-diameter (peeled) Cedar logs *for side eaves*
14	12'	3"-diameter (peeled) Cedar logs *for front & back eaves*
4	8'	3"-diameter (peeled) Cedar logs *for hip corners & rafters*
24	10'	2"-diameter (peeled) Cedar logs *for roof nailers*

FRAME

1	10'	2×10 pressure-treated lumber *for girder*
2	12'	2×10 pressure-treated lumber *for girders & support*
2	10'	2×8 pressure-treated lumber *for joist headers*
4	7'	2×8 pressure-treated lumber *for joists*
1	12'	2×8 pressure-treated lumber *for rear joist header*
2	10'	2×8 pressure-treated lumber *for joists*
2	14'	2×8 pressure-treated lumber *for joists*
4	12'	2×4 pressure-treated lumber *for front & rear plates*
2	14'	2×4 pressure-treated lumber *for side plates*
6	12'	2×4 pressure-treated lumber *for studs*
2	14'	2×4 pressure-treated *for window framing, etc.*
2	10'	4"-wide split bamboo *for the ridge*
2	6'	4"-wide split bamboo *for the hips*
20'		1"-diameter Hempex *rope for stairs*
100'		½"-diameter Hempex *rope for stairs*
500'		⅝" Hempex rope *for railings*
3 rolls		30"×57' palm thatch *for roofing*

SIDING

6	4'×8'	½" mahogany plywood *for sheathing*
4	4'×8'	½" mahogany plywood *for roof*
154 sq. ft.		18" bark shingles *for exterior wall sheathing**

Note: Cut shingles in half crosswise and overlap by minimum of 2"

Note: Source—Parton Lumber 800-624-1501 or 828-287-4257

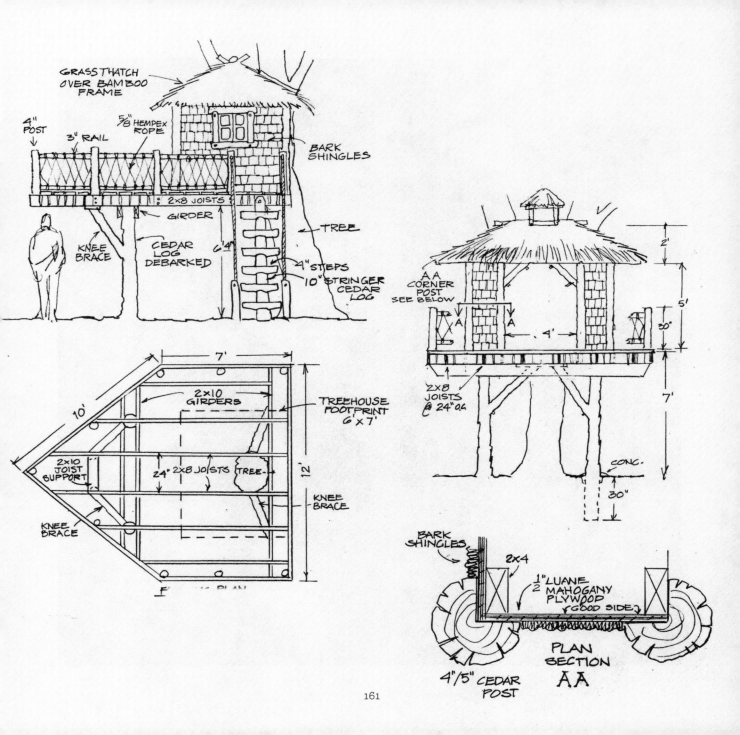

GRASS THATCH OVER BAMBOO FRAME

4" POST

3" RAIL

5/8" HEMPEX ROPE

BARK SHINGLES

2×8 JOISTS

GIRDER

KNEE BRACE

CEDAR LOG DEBARKED

6'4"

TREE

4" STEPS

10" STRINGER CEDAR LOG

7'

10'

2×10 GIRDERS

TREEHOUSE FOOTPRINT 6'×7'

2×10 JOIST SUPPORT

24" 2×8 JOISTS

TREE

KNEE BRACE

KNEE BRACE

12'

PLAN

AA CORNER POST SEE BELOW

A A

4'

2×8 JOISTS @ 24" O.C.

2'

5'

30"

7'

CONC.

30"

BARK SHINGLES

2×4

1/2" LUANE MAHOGANY PLYWOOD (GOOD SIDE)

4"/5" CEDAR POST

PLAN SECTION AA

161

Although glamorous Hollywood sounds an unlikely place for it, the owners of this treehouse wanted it to look like the hut Robinson Crusoe built out of material salvaged from the shipwreck. The deck is shaped like a ship's prow—it gives the owners a grand view of their property. We carved and shaped all the timbers to look as if they'd washed ashore. All the timbers were resurfaced with an adze, and joined with wooden pegs in true Crusoe fashion. We knew the resourceful castaway would have salvaged all the ship's lines (rope) for future use, so we used rope railings wherever possible. The roof was made out of bamboo poles and grass thatch—just the type of materials he would have found on his island. Daniel Defoe's novel *Robinson Crusoe*, first published in 1719, is based on a true story—and we gave the clients' children a condensed version of the book, so they could relive the story in their very own treehouse.

Tree Collar

We chose to incorporate the tree into the structure of the treehouse, so we had to allow for the tree's movement in heavy winds. We built a frame around the branch or trunk, allowing at least 2" clearance for the tree's growth and movement and covered the frame with two pieces of plywood.

An old tire inner tube makes a good weatherproof, flexible collar around the branch. Cut the tube, and nail or staple it to the roof and the tree. Caulk with silicone sealer where the tube meets the tree.

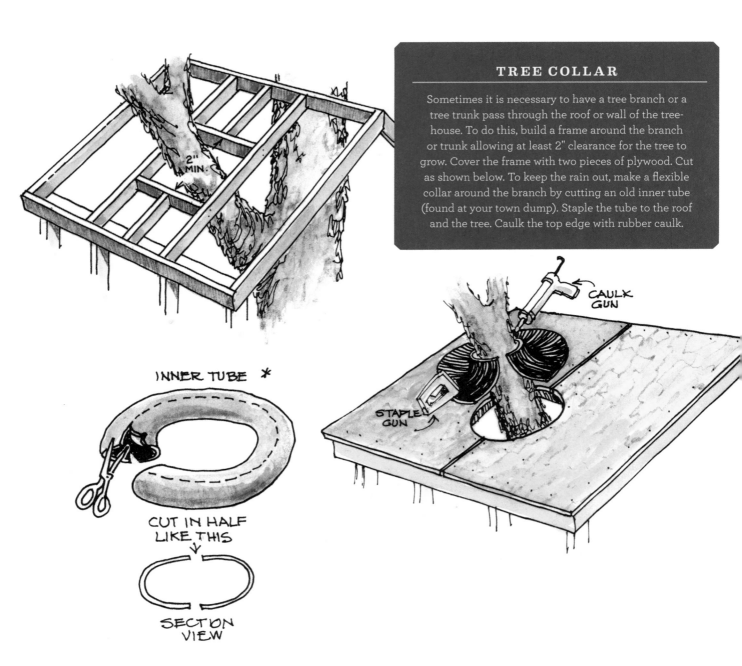

2" MIN.

TREE COLLAR

Sometimes it is necessary to have a tree branch or a tree trunk pass through the roof or wall of the treehouse. To do this, build a frame around the branch or trunk allowing at least 2" clearance for the tree to grow. Cover the frame with two pieces of plywood. Cut as shown below. To keep the rain out, make a flexible collar around the branch by cutting an old inner tube (found at your town dump). Staple the tube to the roof and the tree. Caulk the top edge with rubber caulk.

CAULK GUN

STAPLE GUN

INNER TUBE *

CUT IN HALF LIKE THIS

SECTION VIEW

Single-Stringer Stairs

The stairs are made from half-logs secured to a larger log with strong lag bolts. This set of stairs requires only one stringer: a 10"-diameter log with the butt end securely embedded in the ground. The steps (treads) are pressure-treated 2×10s, supported by 4"-diameter half-logs mortised into the stringer. Attach the rope railings to 4"-diameter posts at the head and foot of the stairs, loop a ½" rope around the railing and screw it to the treads. To prevent the top loops from slipping down the railing, pry open the strands of the 1" rope, and tie a piece of nylon string to both ropes.

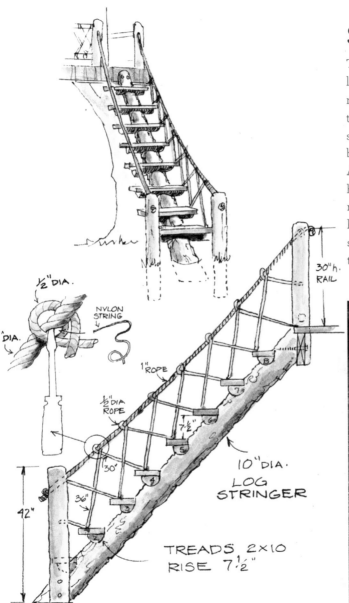

½" DIA.

NYLON STRING

"DIA.

1" ROPE

½" DIA ROPE

30"h. RAIL

30"

36"

42"

7½"

10" DIA. LOG STRINGER

TREADS 2×10 RISE 7½"

Log Window

The windows are framed with small half-round logs (in keeping with the shipwreck theme) and secured with wooden pegs. This inward-opening window is made from ¾" MDO plywood, which is used by highway departments for road signs because of its durability in all weathers. To make the lites (openings), remove the corners with a ¾" spade drill, and cut between the circles with an electric jigsaw. Sand or rout the edges smooth. For safety reasons, we prefer to leave this particular window unglazed. The window is framed with 4" half-logs held in place by ½" wooden pegs.

Kids love anything they can operate, and will enjoy opening this window with its latch and handmade wooden pulls.

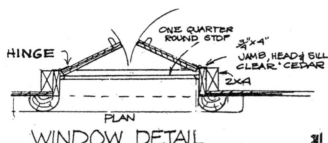

HINGE

ONE QUARTER ROUND STOP

¾" x 4" JAMB, HEAD & SILL CLEAR CEDAR

2 x 4

PLAN

WINDOW DETAIL

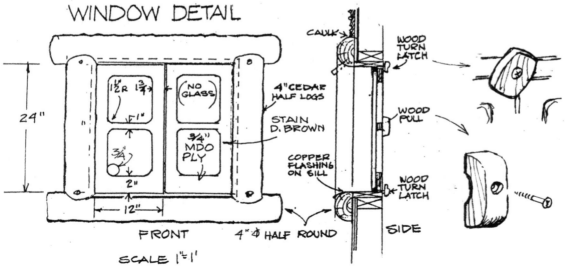

24"

1½ R 1¾

F 1"

NO GLASS

¾"

¾" MDO PLY

2"

12"

FRONT

4" Ø HALF ROUND

SCALE 1"=1'

CAULK

4" CEDAR HALF LOGS

STAIN D. BROWN

COPPER FLASHING ON SILL

WOOD TURN LATCH

WOOD PULL

WOOD TURN LATCH

SIDE

There's a hand-made ladder up to the thatched lookout (or crow's nest!), and a pulley so the castaways can haul in important messages and ship's rations. Robinson Crusoe would have been proud of us.

Two-Tree Treehouse

If you are lucky enough to have two strong trees approximately twelve feet apart, you can build a treehouse like this. We call it a "double-ender" because the front and the back are equally important—great from a child's point of view since it affords maximum visibility. No treehouse is complete without a bucket attached to a rope and pulley. Use this first to life tools up to the platform during construction. Later on, it can be filled with well-deserved refreshments.

MATERIALS

4 12' 2×10 pressure-treated lumber *for double girders (tree span)**

4 8' 2×8 pressure-treated lumber *for headers & floor frame*

4 4' 4×4 pressure-treated lumber *for V-braces (tree to floor frame)*

5 8' 2×8 pressure-treated lumber *for floor joists*

16 8' ⁵⁄₄×6 pressure-treated lumber *for the floor*

4 6' 4×4 #2 cedar *for deck to roof support posts*

4 3' 4×4 #2 cedar *for corner posts*

8 2' 2×4 #2 cedar *for braces*

2 8' 2×8 #2 fir *for roof purlins*

Note: fir & pine should be treated with clear preservative for outdoor use

2 5' 2×8 #2 fir *for roof cross-supports*

7 4' 2×6 #2 fir *for roof rafters*

16 8' 1×6 #2 pine tongue & groove *for roof*

1 36" roll rolled roofing *for roof*

2 8' 2×4 #2 cedar *for sidewalls*

16 28" 1×6 #2 cedar *for sidewalls*

6 3"-diameter 8' poles *for rails*

1 4'×4' ½" plywood *for gusset plates*

300' ⅝" Hempex rope *for rails*

2 36" ¾" nylon rope *for girder retainers*

4 1"×5" stainless-steel threaded rod *for girder supports*

4 ½"×6" galvanized lag screws *for V-brace to trees*

8 ½"×5" galvanized lag screws *for V-brace to floor*

8 ½"×4" galvanized lag screws *for corner posts*

* Adjust length to your tree span.

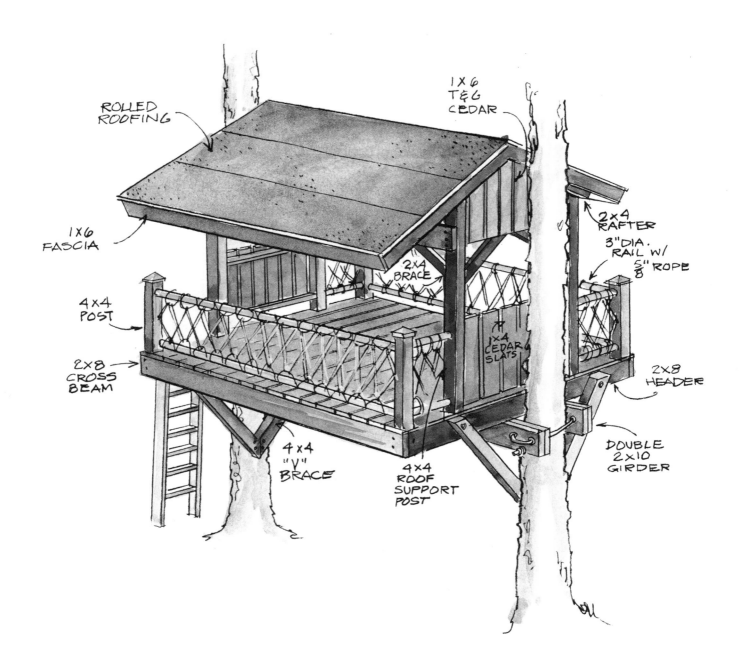

ROLLED
ROOFING

1X6
T&G
CEDAR

1X6
FASCIA

2X4
RAFTER

3"DIA.
RAIL W/
5/8" ROPE

2X4
BRACE

4X4
POST

1X6
CEDAR
SLATS

2X8
CROSS
BEAM

2X8
HEADER

4X4
"V"
BRACE

4X4
ROOF
SUPPORT
POST

DOUBLE
2X10
GIRDER

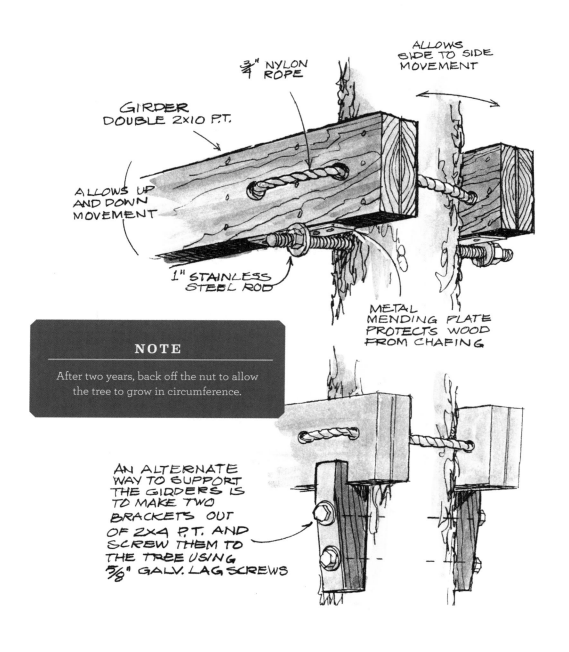

¾" NYLON ROPE

ALLOWS SIDE TO SIDE MOVEMENT

GIRDER DOUBLE 2x10 P.T.

ALLOWS UP AND DOWN MOVEMENT

1" STAINLESS STEEL ROD

METAL MENDING PLATE PROTECTS WOOD FROM CHAFING

NOTE

After two years, back off the nut to allow the tree to grow in circumference.

AN ALTERNATE WAY TO SUPPORT THE GIDDERS IS TO MAKE TWO BRACKETS OUT OF 2x4 P.T. AND SCREW THEM TO THE TREE USING ⅝" GALV. LAG SCREWS

The treehouse is supported by girders under the floor joists, and by "V" braces under the side headers.

We spanned the trees with doubled 2×10 pressure-treated girders on either side of the tree trunks; the ends rest on 1"-diameter stainless-steel rods drilled into the trunks, to allow the trees to flex in the wind. A length of ¾" nylon rope runs through holes in the ends of the girders to hold them close to the trees.

The 8'-square platform does not touch or hinder the trees, and is supported by a V-brace on each end. The braces are attached to the trees with ½" lag screws, and bolted to the floor frame with ½" galvanized bolts.

The floor (deck) frame is made of 2×8 pressure-treated lumber. The two side headers were attached first, then the front and rear cross-beams, and finally the 2×8 pressure-treated joists which fit between the cross-beams on 16" centers.

The ⁵⁄₄×6 pressure-treated deck boards are notched at the corners for the 4×4 pressure-treated corner posts and the roof support posts. The boards are spaced ½" apart.

The roof rests on horizontal 2×8 pressure-treated

cross-beams, attached to the outside face of the roof support posts and reinforced with 2×4 braces. Two 2×6 roof trusses were made on the deck and lifted up onto the beams. There is a bird's-mouth notch where the truss rests on the beam. We copied this onto six more 2×6 trusses, installed at 16" centers. The roof is made of 1×6 T&G boards, nailed to the rafters and covered with rolled roofing. 1×6 fascia boards give a finishing touch.

The railings are 3"-diameter poles, with ⅝" Hempex rope (from R&W Rope Suppliers) woven around the top and bottom rails. The side railings are cedar 2×4s screwed across the inside of the roof support posts, with 1×4 cedar slats attached.

In 2012, this treehouse was put to the ultimate test of 70–80mph winds coming off the ocean in Hurricane Sandy. It survived without a scratch.

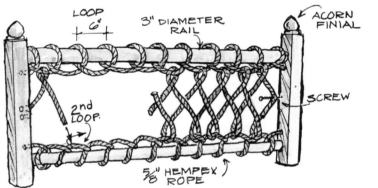

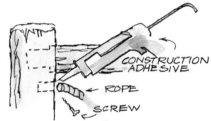

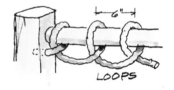

Rope Railing

Drill a hole, slightly larger than the diameter of the rope and just below the top rail, in the first post. Squeeze a small amount of polyurethane construction adhesive into the hole, and insert the end of the rope. Secure it with a 2½" screw, driven at an angle through the rope. (See above right).

Feed the rope under and over the rail, and behind the loop, before proceeding to the next loop. Continue making 6"-wide loops until you reach the next post. Attach to the post as before, and repeat on the bottom rail.

Attach the next rope to the mid-point of the first post. Thread the rope through the first loop on the top rail and down through the second loop on the bottom rail.

Continue threading the rope through every other loop until you reach the second post. Screw the rope midway to the post and continue threading back through the loops until you reach the end. Cut the rope and attach as in Step 1.

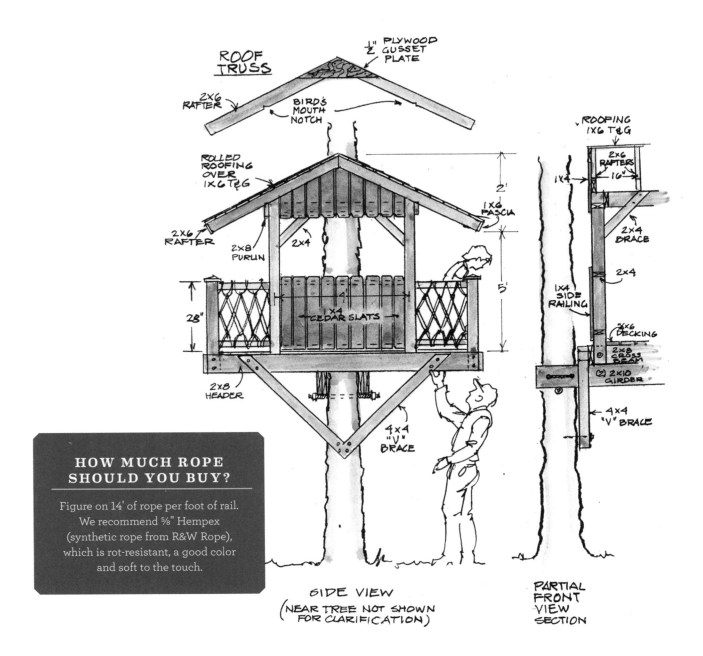

ROOF
TRUSS

½" PLYWOOD
GUSSET
PLATE

2X6
RAFTER

BIRD'S
MOUTH
NOTCH

ROLLED
ROOFING
OVER
1X6 T&G

1X6
FASCIA

2X6
RAFTER

2X4

2X8
PURLIN

28"

4'

1X4
CEDAR SLATS

5'

2X8
HEADER

4X4
"V"
BRACE

2'

ROOFING
1X6 T&G

2X6
RAFTERS

16"

1X4

2X4
BRACE

2X4

1X4
SIDE
RAILING

2X6
DECKING

2X8
CROSS
BEAM

(2) 2X10
GIRDER

4X4
"V" BRACE

**HOW MUCH ROPE
SHOULD YOU BUY?**

Figure on 14' of rope per foot of rail.
We recommend ⅝" Hempex
(synthetic rope from R&W Rope),
which is rot-resistant, a good color
and soft to the touch.

SIDE VIEW
(NEAR TREE NOT SHOWN
FOR CLARIFICATION)

PARTIAL
FRONT
VIEW
SECTION

Three-Legged Treehouse

If you have no trees, don't worry: the three-legged treehouse or fort is easily built using three pressure-treated posts instead of trees. Part of its popularity is that it can be constructed in one afternoon at minimal cost—we even constructed one in Rockefeller Center during a three-hour segment of *The Today Show* on NBC. It is an easy hideaway for kids, and can later be transformed into a pool pump/filter enclosure or even a bell tower.

MATERIALS

3 10' 2×8 fir *for floor beams and roof beams*

Note: fir & pine should be treated with clear preservative for outdoor use

3 6"-diameter 8' pressure-treated posts *for corner posts*

1 10' 1×2 #2 pine *for floor beam*

2 4'×8' ⅝" exterior plywood *for floor and roof*

1 8' 2×4 #2 fir *for door post*

3 10' 2×4 #2 fir *for railings*

6 8' 1×4 #2 pine *for railing slats*

1 10' 2×6 #2 fir *for stair legs*

1 8' 2×6 #2 fir *for stair treads*

2 8' 2×4 #2 fir *for stair rails and railing posts*

1 8' 1×4 #2 pine *for support cleats*

26 ½"×4" galvanized lag screws and washers

16 ⅜"×4" galvanized lag screws and washers

8 ⅜"×3½" galvanized carriage bolts

1lb. 8d galvanized finishing nails

1 box 2" galvanized deck screws

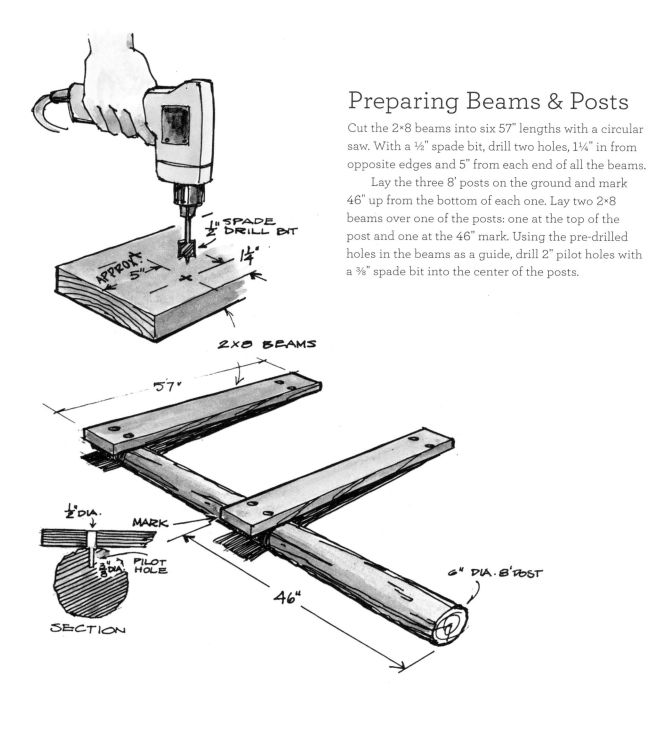

Preparing Beams & Posts

Cut the 2×8 beams into six 57" lengths with a circular saw. With a ½" spade bit, drill two holes, 1¼" in from opposite edges and 5" from each end of all the beams.

Lay the three 8' posts on the ground and mark 46" up from the bottom of each one. Lay two 2×8 beams over one of the posts: one at the top of the post and one at the 46" mark. Using the pre-drilled holes in the beams as a guide, drill 2" pilot holes with a ⅜" spade bit into the center of the posts.

½" SPADE DRILL BIT

1¼"

APPROX. 5"

2×8 BEAMS

57"

½" DIA.

MARK

PILOT HOLE

⅜" DIA.

SECTION

46"

6" DIA. 8' POST

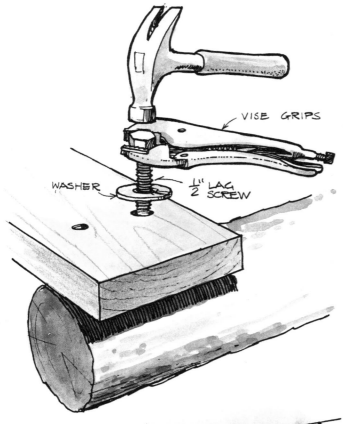

Attaching Beams & Posts

Lock a pair of vise grip pliers onto the head of a ½" lag screw, so that the head protrudes above the pliers by ½". Attach a washer to the screw and start it into one of the holes in the beam by giving the head of the screw a few hard taps with a hammer. Turn the lag screw one revolution at a time between hammer blows; after several revolutions, the threads of the screw will catch the wood, and hammering will no longer be necessary. Screw the lag screw all the way into the beam until you see the washer begin to press into the wood. Repeat the procedure until you have two beams secured to each post.

Floor Support

Turn the post over so that the insides of the beams are facing up. Cut and nail a 40"-long 1×2 floor support to the lower beam, ¾" below the top edge and 10" from the open end. Repeat for the other two posts.

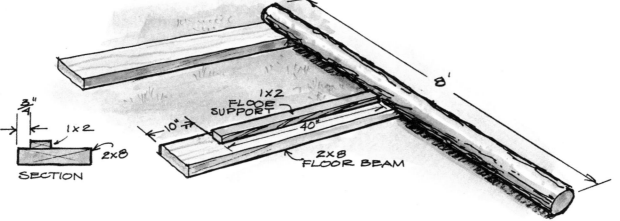

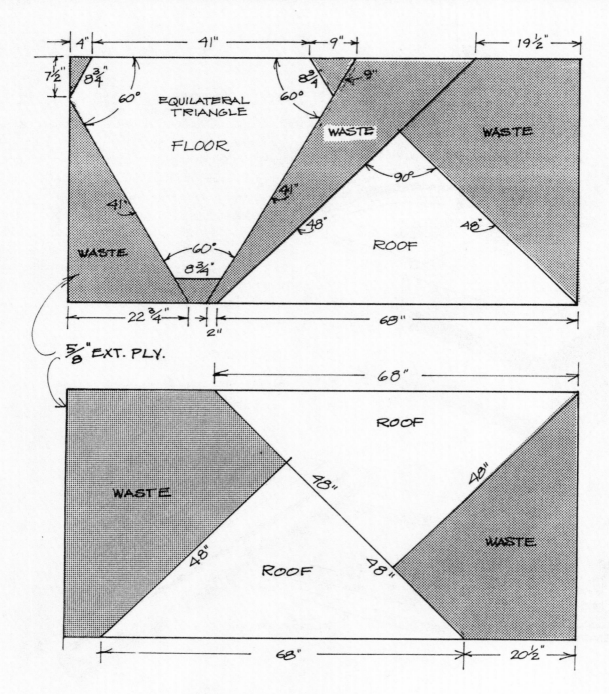

2X8 ROOF BEAM

1X2 FLOOR SUPPORT

3/8 PILOT HOLES

5/8" EXT. PLY FLOOR

Assembly

With the help of two assistants, stand the three posts up and measure for the floor panel: it will be approximately the size shown, but posts are variable in shape and thickness and it's difficult to give precise dimensions here. Cut the floor to fit, and nail it in place, on top of the 1×2 and almost flush with the top of the lower beams.

To secure the unfastened end of each floor beam, drill pilot holes through the pre-drilled beams into the posts and attach using ½" lag screws. Once the lower screws are in place, stand on a stepladder and attach the top beams in the same way.

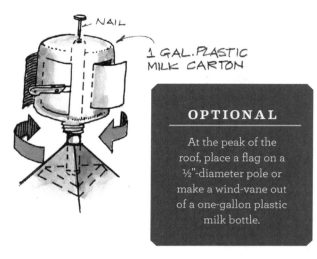

NAIL

1 GAL. PLASTIC MILK CARTON

OPTIONAL

At the peak of the roof, place a flag on a ½"-diameter pole or make a wind-vane out of a one-gallon plastic milk bottle.

Roof

With an assistant, assemble the three plywood roof panels on the ground and join them with 8d finishing nails spaced 6" apart. Lift the roof onto the beams and secure it with 2" deck screws every 6".

Door Post and Railings

To make the door post, cut a 2×4, 57" long; using a jigsaw, cut 1½" × 3½" notches for the railing and 1½" × 7" notches at top and bottom, as shown. Drill two ⅜"-diameter holes in the top and bottom of the post. Measure and mark 30" from the outside edge of the 2×8 roof and floor beams. Line up the stair-side face of the doorpost with the marks. Screw the doorpost to the upper and lower beams with ⅜" × 4" lag screws.

To construct the railings beside the stairs, cut two pieces of 2×4, 30" long, and screw them into the door post notches and the left corner post with ⅜" × 4" lag screws. For the other two sides, cut four more 2×4s 5' long, and screw them to the outside of the posts at the same height.

Nail 1×4 railing slats to the inside of the tree-house railing at 1" intervals. Allow the slats to protrude at least 1" above the top of the railing. Sand the edges to round off any sharp corners.

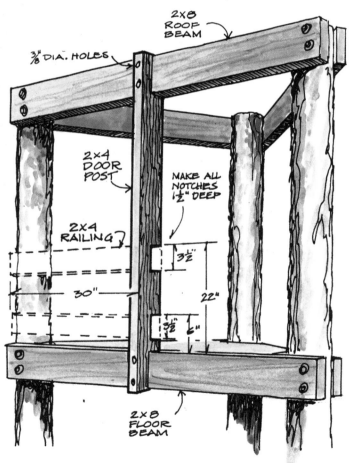

⅜" DIA. HOLES

2×8 ROOF BEAM

2×4 DOOR POST

2×4 RAILING

MAKE ALL NOTCHES 1½" DEEP

3½"

30"

3½" 6"

22"

2×8 FLOOR BEAM

Stairs

Dig two small holes in which the ladder legs can rest. Cut a 2×6 into two 5' lengths for the legs. Cut a bird's mouth notch at the top of each leg to fit the floor beam. Attach the top of the legs to the floor beam using ½"×4" lag screws. Position the bottom of each leg in the holes.

Use a circular saw to cut five 16"-long treads from 2×6. Cut 10 angled support cleats for the steps from 1×4.

Starting from the bottom up, screw two support cleats to the inside of the legs using 1¼" deck screws (three screws per cleat). Nail two 10d nails through the leg into the tread on each side. Continue this sequence until you reach the platform.

For an extra safe stairway, add a railing: cut the railing and posts out of 2×4 and attach them, using ⅜"×3½" carriage bolts. Use ½"×4" lag screws to join the top of the stair railings to the doorpost and the corner post.

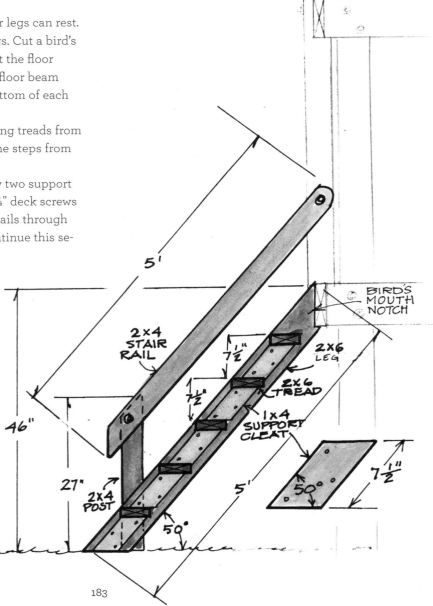

5'

BIRD'S MOUTH NOTCH

2×4 STAIR RAIL

7½"

7½"

2×6 LEG

2×6 TREAD

1×4 SUPPORT CLEAT

46"

27"

2×4 POST

50°

5'

50°

7½"

Traditional Playhouse

At six feet by six feet, this playhouse is small enough to prefabricate in a basement or workshop and move in sections to the final site. It's a great playhouse in which kids can practice their interior-decorating skills. Serious house dwellers might want to keep battery-operated lights and a cordless telephone inside; thrift-shop furniture or packing crates can be decorated and arranged artfully, and fabric remnants or tea towels are easy to hang from a curtain rod.

MATERIALS

2   8"×16"×4" solid concrete blocks *for corners*

3   12'   2×4 pressure-treated lumber *for floor frame & floor joists*

1   4'×8'   ¾" A-D plywood *for interior floor & door*

2   12'   ⁵⁄₄×6 pressure-treated lumber *for exterior decking*

1   6'   1" half-round molding *for deck edging*

2   8'   4×4 posts *for porch posts*

16   8'   2×4 #2 fir *for wall studs, side wall bottom plates, roof rafters, & bottom porch railing*

Note: fir & pine should be treated with clear preservative for outdoor use

6   12'   2×4 #2 fir *for top plates, front wall bottom plate, & back wall bottom plate*

2   4'×8'   ½" CDX plywood for roof and gusset plates

12   8'   1×4 #2 pine *for ridge pole, gable ends, corner post trim, door trim, gable trim, & roof ridge trim*

205 linear ft.   ½"×6" clapboard *for wall siding*

4   10'   1×6 #2 cedar tongue and groove *for gables*

1   14'   1×4 #2 pine *for fascia boards*

4   8'   1×2 #2 pine *for gable trim & doorstop*

3 boxes 3"-wide round-bottom fancy-cut cedar shingles *for roof*

4   8'   2×2 clear cedar *for balusters*

1   8' cedar railing *for porch*

2   1½"×3' galvanized hinges *for door*

2   5" handles *for door*

2   Decorative black strap hinges *for door*

4   18"×18" windows with 4 lites

8   6"×18" decorative shutters *for windows*

4   Decorative brackets *for porch*

1 gallon paint

Nails

1lb.   6d galvanized common nails

2lbs.   20d galvanized common nails

3lbs.   10d galvanized common nails

3lbs.   3d galvanized shingling nails

3lbs.   6d galvanized siding nails

1lb.   8d galvanized finishing nails

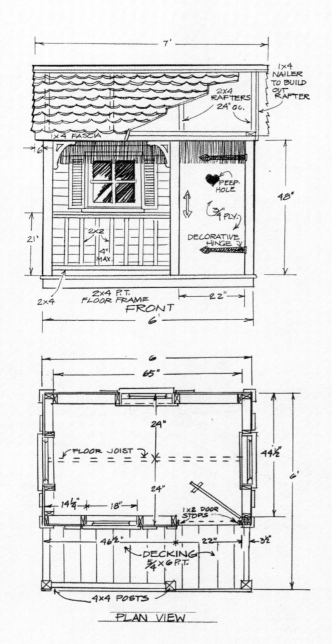

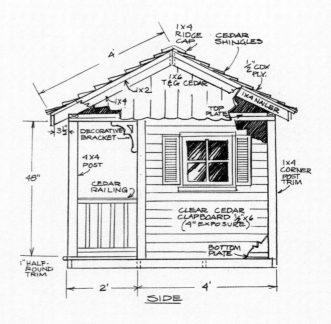

FRONT

7'

1x4 NAILER TO BUILD OUT RAFTER

2x4 RAFTERS 24" O.C.

1x4 FASCIA

6"

PEEP-HOLE

48"

3/4" PLY.

DECORATIVE HINGE

2x2

4" MAX.

21"

DECORATIVE BRACKET

2x4

2x4 P.T. FLOOR FRAME

22"

6'

SIDE

1x4 RIDGE CAP

CEDAR SHINGLES

1/2" CDX PLY.

4'

1x6 T&G CEDAR

1x2

1x4

TOP PLATE

1x4 NAILER

3 1/2"

DECORATIVE BRACKET

4x4 POST

CEDAR RAILING

48"

1x4 CORNER POST TRIM

CLEAR CEDAR CLAPBOARD 1/2"x6 (4" EXPOSURE)

BOTTOM PLATE

1" HALF-ROUND TRIM

2'

4'

PLAN VIEW

6

65"

24"

FLOOR JOIST

44 1/2"

6'

24"

1x2 DOOR STOPS

14 1/8"

18"

46 1/2"

22"

3 1/2"

DECKING 5/4 x 6 P.T.

4x4 POSTS

Base

Clear the area where you want the playhouse to go. Build a 6'×6' frame for the floor by cutting pressure-treated 2×4s with a circular saw and nailing them together with 10d nails.

Mark and cut two 69" 2×4 floor joists and, using 20d common nails, nail them at 24" centers. Cut a piece of ¾" A-D plywood to 4'×6'. Lay the plywood on top of the floor frame, using the plywood as a guide to check that the corners of the floor frame are square. Using 6d siding nails, nail the plywood to the frame and joists.

Nail the pressure-treated ⁵⁄₄×6 decking to the porch floor frame, positioning it perpendicular to the front wall of the playhouse. Trim the front edge of the decking with half-round molding, nailed in place with 6d siding nails.

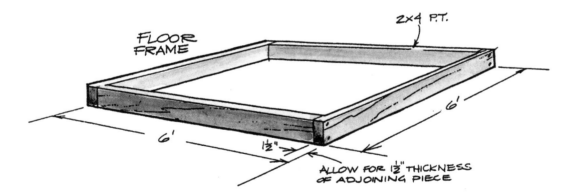

FLOOR FRAME

2×4 P.T.

6'

6'

1½"

ALLOW FOR 1½" THICKNESS OF ADJOINING PIECE

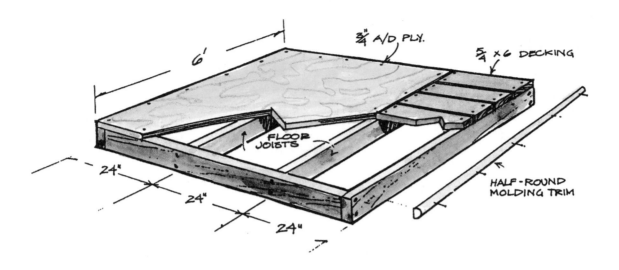

6'

¾" A/D PLY.

⅝ ×6 DECKING

FLOOR JOISTS

HALF-ROUND MOLDING TRIM

24"

24"

24"

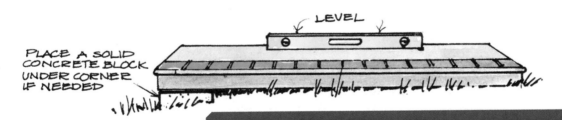

LEVEL

PLACE A SOLID CONCRETE BLOCK UNDER CORNER IF NEEDED

BUILDING TIP

Building sites are seldom level. A good way to level the base of this structure is to place 8"×16"×4" solid concrete blocks under the low end. Make sure the blocks rest on compacted soil and that the floor is absolutely level, since this will affect the construction of the whole playhouse.

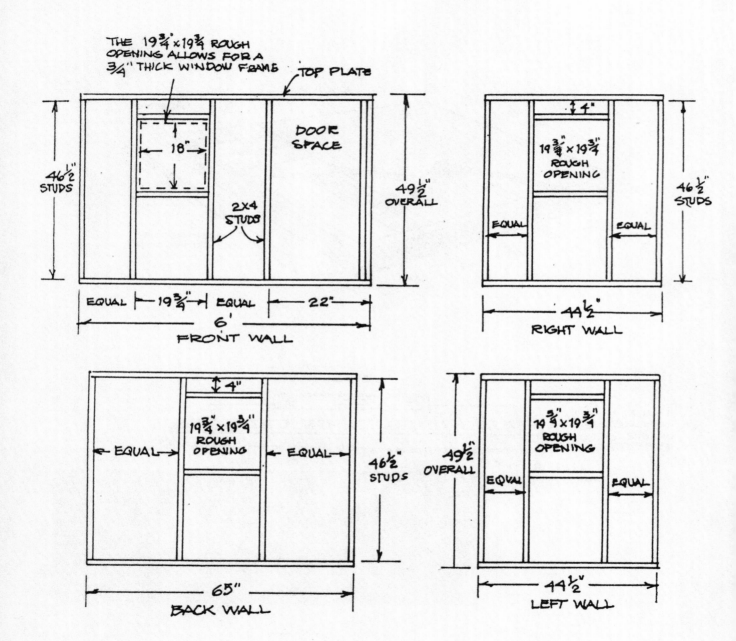

THE 19¾" × 19¾" ROUGH OPENING ALLOWS FOR A ¾" THICK WINDOW FRAME

TOP PLATE

DOOR SPACE

18"

2X4 STUDS

46½" STUDS

49½" OVERALL

EQUAL   19¾"   EQUAL   22"

6'

FRONT WALL

4"

19¾" × 19¾" ROUGH OPENING

EQUAL   EQUAL

46½" STUDS

44½"

RIGHT WALL

4"

19¾" × 19¾" ROUGH OPENING

EQUAL   EQUAL

46½" STUDS

65"

BACK WALL

19¾" × 19¾" ROUGH OPENING

EQUAL   EQUAL

49½" OVERALL

44½"

LEFT WALL

Framing

Cut two 8' 4×4 fir posts into 48" lengths. Toenail three of these to the decking using 8d finishing nails, as shown.

Construct each of the four walls separately, using the playhouse floor as a level workspace. Use a temporary prop to hold the first wall in place while you nail the single-layer bottom plate to the floor with 10d common nails. Note that the porch does not have a bottom plate. After each wall is completed, tilt it into place and nail it to the adjoining wall using 10d common nails.

After the walls are completed, nail the first layer of the 2×4 top plate onto the porch posts, and toenail it into the first layer of the wall top plate using 10d nails. Attach a second top plate to the first layer of all four sides and the porch, staggering all joints.

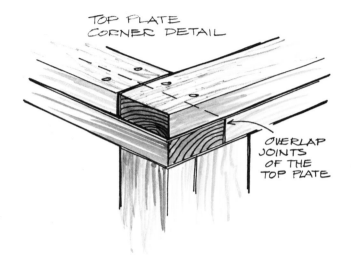

TOP PLATE
CORNER DETAIL

OVERLAP
JOINTS
OF THE
TOP PLATE

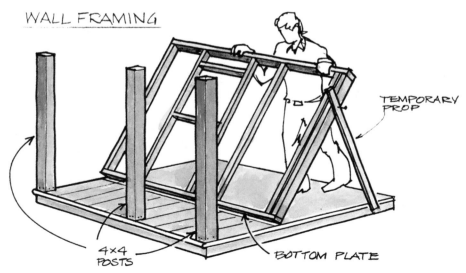

WALL FRAMING

TEMPORARY
PROP

4×4
POSTS

BOTTOM PLATE

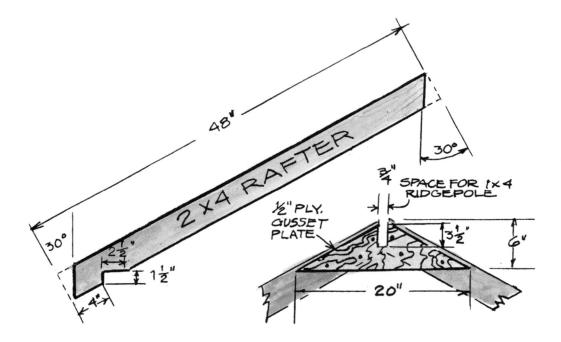

Rafters

To make the roof rafters, cut four 8' 2×4s in half. Using a protractor, mark a 30-degree angle on each end of the 4' rafters, and cut at this angle. Make a 1½"×2½" notch 4" from the bottom end of each rafter. This notch allows the bottom of the rafter to rest securely on top of the top plate.

Cut each CDX plywood panel to 4'×7' for the roof, and set aside. From the leftover plywood, cut eight notched gusset plates as shown in the illustration.

To join the peaks of the rafters, nail a gusset plate to each side of the rafters, leaving a ¾" space for the 1×4 ridge pole. Lift the paired rafters into position (at 24" centers) and slip the 7' ridgepole into the rafter notches. Toenail the bottom of the rafters to the top plates using 6d common nails. Check that the rafters are plumb, and toenail the peaks to the ridge pole.

Roofing and Siding

Nail the pre-cut plywood roof panels to the rafters, using 6d common nails every 6". Cut ½"×6" clear cedar clapboards to fit the walls of the playhouse, and attach using 6d siding nails. Overlap the boards so that 4" of each is exposed. Finish off the ends of the siding by nailing 1×4 corner post trim to the outside edges of the corners, using 6d siding nails.

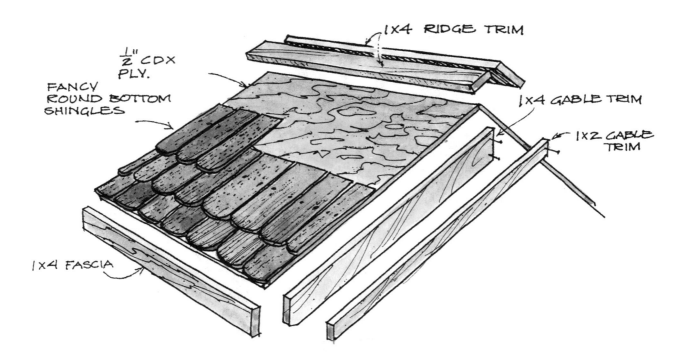

1×4 RIDGE TRIM

½" CDX PLY.

FANCY ROUND BOTTOM SHINGLES

1×4 GABLE TRIM

1×2 GABLE TRIM

1×4 FASCIA

Gable Ends and Trim

Nail the pre-cut plywood roof panels to the rafters, using 6d common nails every 6". Cut ½"×6" clear cedar clapboards to fit the walls of the playhouse, and attach using 6d siding nails. Overlap the boards so that 4" of each is exposed. Finish off the ends of the siding by nailing 1×4 corner post trim to the outside edges of the corners, using 6d siding nails.

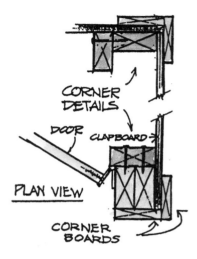

CORNER
DETAILS

DOOR   CLAPBOARD

<u>PLAN VIEW</u>

CORNER
BOARDS

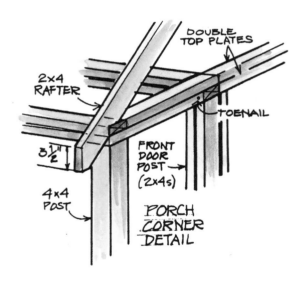

DOUBLE
TOP PLATES

2×4
RAFTER

TOENAIL

3½"

FRONT
DOOR
POST
(2×4s)

4×4
POST

PORCH
CORNER
DETAIL

BUILD OUT
RAFTER AND
TOP PLATES
WITH 1×4S

T&G
1×6

1×4

1×4

1×4

1×4

CORNER
BOARDS

Fascia Boards & Shingles

For the fascia boards, cut a 14' 1×4 in half, and nail the boards to the front and rear eaves of the roof. Nail 1×2 gable trim on top of the 1×4 gable trim. Attach the shingles with 3d shingling nails, so that the nails don't protrude through the plywood into the playhouse. Nail the 1×4 ridge trim to the peak, using finishing nails.

Porch

For the bottom railing, cut an 8' 2×4 to fit between the porch posts (along the front) and between the post and the wall (along the sides). Cut five balusters of equal length from each 8' 2×2. Space seven balusters equally between the porch posts and mark their locations on the 2×4. Position the balusters along the marks and nail through the 2×4 bottom railing into the end of the 2×2 balusters with 8d finishing nails. After all the balusters have been attached, toenail this assembly to the two posts, leaving a 2" space between the decking and the 2×4 bottom railing.

Using finishing nails and nailing from underneath the railing, toenail the balusters to the cedar railing, and this top railing to the posts. Do the same for the side railings, using four balusters on each side—toenailing one end to the porch posts, and the other to the front wall.

Door

The door is made from ¾" plywood left over from the floor. Cut it to fit the opening, and cut a heart-shaped peephole in the center. Since we have designed the door to swing inward, mount the hinges on the inside of the playhouse.

Provide a stop for the door by nailing a 1×2 to each side and along the top of the door frame. Attach a handle to each side of the door. For decoration, attach two fake strap hinges to the front of the door. Nail on the 1×4 door trim, using finishing nails. Attach shutters and brackets according to the manufacturer's instructions. For easy-to-make windows, see *Hexagonal Garden House—Windows* page 108.

Garden Playhouse

This open-air playhouse, made of lattice and canvas, makes a wonderful garden retreat in which your kids can practice being junior gardeners. They can get seeds started, put together bouquets for tea parties and lemonade breaks, meet with their friends or just use it as a quiet place to read or do their homework. Plant roses or clematis to grow up the trellis walls, weave the stems through the openings and soon this garden playhouse will look as if made of blossoms—perfect for a sunny spot at the end of a winding path.

MATERIALS

2 10' 6×6 pressure-treated lumber *for base*

½ cu. yd. builder's sand

100 4"×8" used bricks *for base*

8 8' 2×4 pressure-treated lumber *for posts*

14 12' 2×2 pressure-treated lumber *for horizontal lattice frame*

4 10' 2×4 pressure-treated lumber *for top plates*

2 4'×8' ¾" exterior plywood *for roof*

1 8' ¾"×¾" quarter-round molding *for roof*

1 6'×9' 12oz. duck canvas with selvage *for roof covering*

2 8' 3/8"-diameter wooden poles *for roof*

2 4'×8' diagonal cedar lattice *for walls*

1 4'×8' perpendicular lattice *for gables*

12 8' 1×4 pressure-treated lumber *for door trim & corner trim*

1 10' 1×4 cedar *for frieze board*

1 10' ⅞"×1⅛" nose & cove molding *for gables*

2 8' ¹¹⁄₁₆"×1⅜" solid crown molding *for gables*

2 12' 2×2 pressure-treated lumber *for gable lattice frame*

1 4'×4' ¾" marine plywood *for brackets*

Monel construction staples *for roof*

1 gallon semi-gloss enamel paint

FASTENERS

1 lb. 3d galvanized common nails

1 lb. 6d galvanized common nails

1 lb. 8d galvanized finishing nails

1 lb. 4d galvanized finishing nails

1 lb. 2½" galvanized deck screws

1 box ½" staples

8 40d galvanized common nails

8 ¼"×4" galvanized lag screws

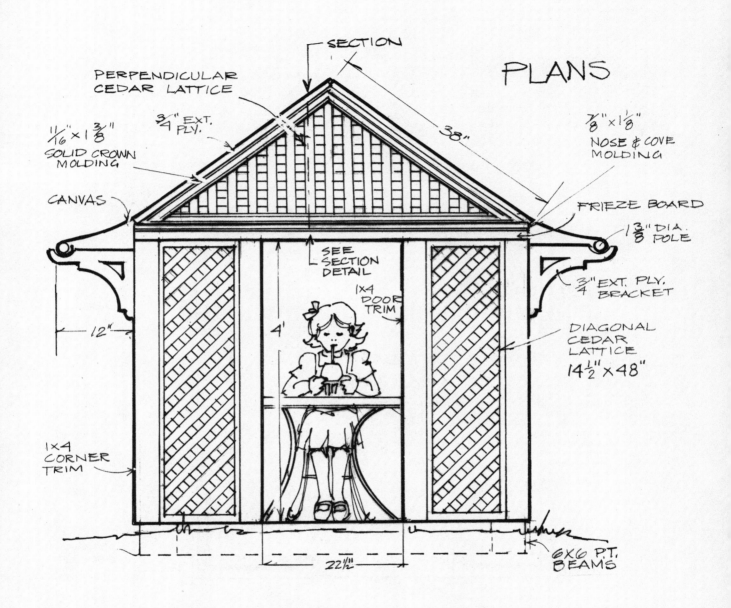

SECTION

PLANS

PERPENDICULAR
CEDAR LATTICE

3/4" EXT.
PLY.

$\frac{11}{16}$" × 1$\frac{3}{8}$"
SOLID CROWN
MOLDING

38"

$\frac{7}{8}$" × 1$\frac{1}{8}$"
NOSE & COVE
MOLDING

FRIEZE BOARD

CANVAS

1$\frac{3}{8}$" DIA.
POLE

SEE
SECTION
DETAIL

1×4
DOOR
TRIM

3/4" EXT. PLY.
BRACKET

12"

4'

DIAGONAL
CEDAR
LATTICE
14$\frac{1}{2}$" × 48"

1×4
CORNER
TRIM

22$\frac{1}{2}$"

6X6 P.T.
BEAMS

FRONT

The following instructions are for a brick and timber base; however, if you want to build a temporary structure that can be easily moved, make the base out of pressure-treated lumber. We recommend using screws rather than nails, so the playhouse can be easily taken apart and reassembled. These dimensions are geared toward children, but could easily be adapted for adults to make a perfect garden shed.

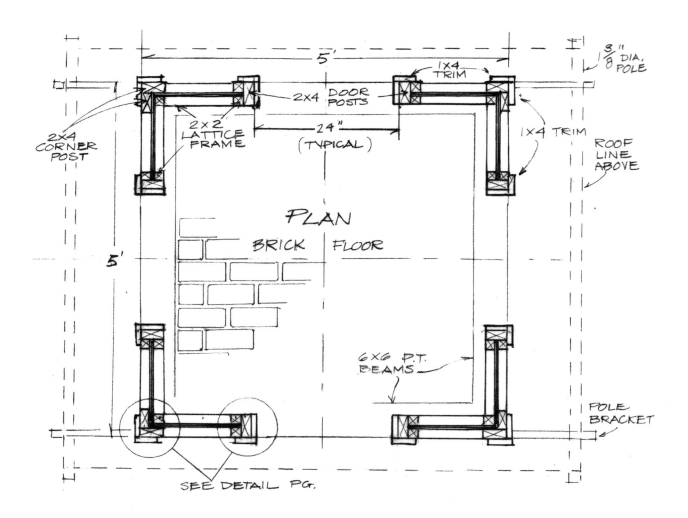

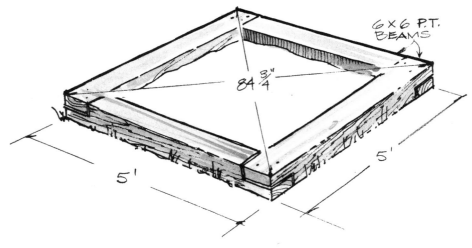

6×6 P.T. BEAMS

84 3/4"

5'

5'

Base

Level a 5'×5' area, removing any large roots and rocks. Cut the 6×6 pressure-treated timbers into four 5' lengths. Join the four beams at the corners, using lap joints.

Place the beams on the prepared site to form a 5' square. Check the diagonals, which should be 84¾". Drive a 40d nail into the center of each corner joint and recheck the diagonals for square. Drive four 10d nails into each joint to hold it in place.

ELECTRIC CIRCULAR SAW

2 3/4"

5 1/2"

MARK

40d NAIL

FOUR 16d NAILS

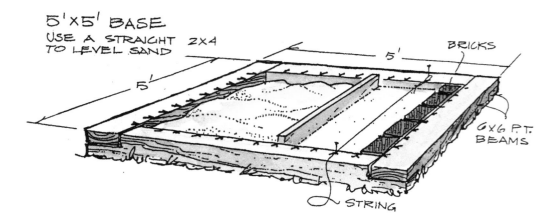

5'×5' BASE
USE A STRAIGHT 2×4
TO LEVEL SAND

5'

5'

BRICKS

6×6 P.T.
BEAMS

STRING

Floor

Fill the frame with sand to within 2" of the top, compressing it as much as possible. Use a straightedge to level the sand, and sprinkle it with water before laying the bricks. Keep the lines of bricks straight with a string line attached to nails in the beams. Stagger the rows, using half bricks where necessary.

Walls

Cut each 8' 2×4 in half. Use two lengths per corner, and one to frame each side of the entrance. To form the corner posts, screw two 2×4s together in an L shape (see corner detail). Stand one post up in the corner and screw it to the base. Follow the same steps for the remaining three posts.

To install the lattice, cut and nail 2×2s flush with the outside edge of the framing, using 8d nails. (Nail the vertical pieces first.) Cut 8 14½"×48" pieces of diagonal cedar lattice, and nail them with 3d nails to the 2×2s from inside the playhouse. Add a second frame of 2×2s on the inside, to secure the lattice.

2½" DECK SCREW

6×6 P.T. BEAM

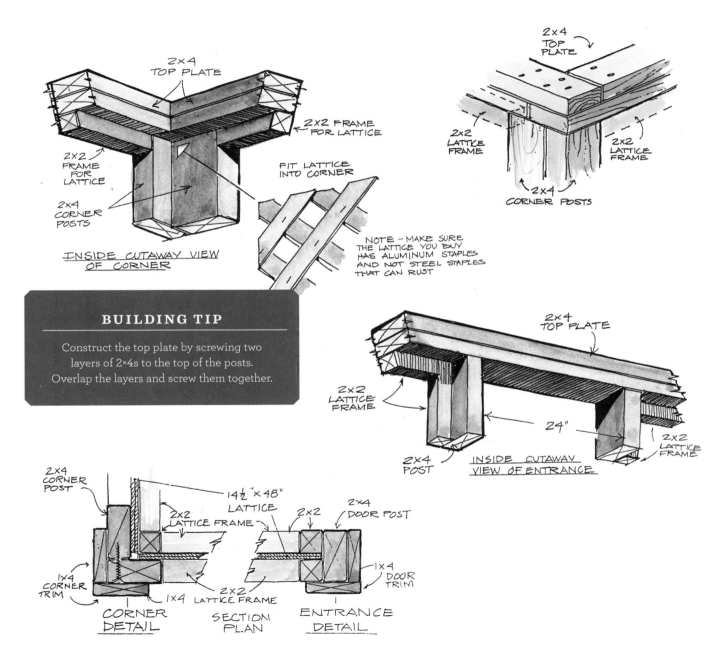

2×4 TOP PLATE

2×2 FRAME FOR LATTICE

2×2 FRAME FOR LATTICE

2×4 CORNER POSTS

INSIDE CUTAWAY VIEW OF CORNER

FIT LATTICE INTO CORNER

NOTE – MAKE SURE THE LATTICE YOU BUY HAS ALUMINUM STAPLES AND NOT STEEL STAPLES THAT CAN RUST

2×4 TOP PLATE

2×2 LATTICE FRAME

2×2 LATTICE FRAME

2×4 CORNER POSTS

BUILDING TIP

Construct the top plate by screwing two layers of 2×4s to the top of the posts. Overlap the layers and screw them together.

2×4 TOP PLATE

2×2 LATTICE FRAME

24"

2×2 LATTICE FRAME

2×4 POST

INSIDE CUTAWAY VIEW OF ENTRANCE

2×4 CORNER POST

1×4 CORNER TRIM

CORNER DETAIL

$14\frac{1}{2}$"×48" LATTICE

2×2 LATTICE FRAME

2×2 LATTICE FRAME

SECTION PLAN

2×2

2×4 DOOR POST

1×4 DOOR TRIM

ENTRANCE DETAIL

Roof

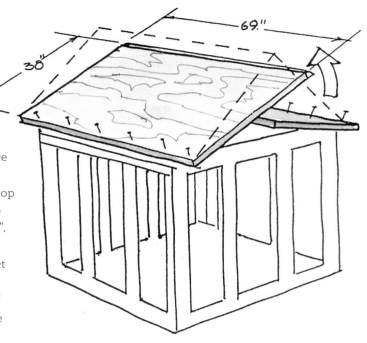

Cut two 38"×69" pieces of ¾" plywood. Lay one piece on top of the wall frame and, using 6d nails, temporarily nail the bottom edge of the roof panel to the top outside edge of the 2×4 wall framing. Make sure the short sides of the plywood overlap the frame by 4½". Repeat this step with the second roof panel.

To make the roof assembly easier and to protect the canvas from chafing, use construction adhesive and 8d finishing nails to glue and nail a 69" strip of quarter-round molding to the top edge of one of the roof panels.

From inside the structure, and with an assistant, push the panels up from the center until they meet at the top. (The temporary nails will bend, and act as hinges.)

Standing on a ladder outside the playhouse, screw the top edges of the roof panels together with 2½" deck screws. Make sure the screw heads are below the surface of the plywood. Screw the bottom edges of the roof panels to the top plates with 2½" deck screws, and remove the temporary nails.

Glue or staple the canvas to the plywood roof, leaving an overhang of 1½" on each side. Staple the overhanging canvas onto 75"-long poles, and turn the poles to wrap the canvas around them.

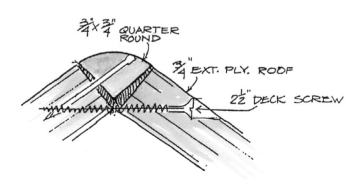

Gable & Door Trim

Trim the edges of the triangular gables with solid crown molding. Nail two 1×4 frieze boards to the edge of the top plates using 8d finishing nails; attach nose & cove molding to the top front of the boards with 4d finishing nails. Cut a piece of perpendicular lattice to fit each gable opening. Install the lattice against the crown molding from the inside, and secure it with cedar 2×2s nailed to the top plate with 8d finishing nails. Trim the corners and the four doorways with 1×4s.

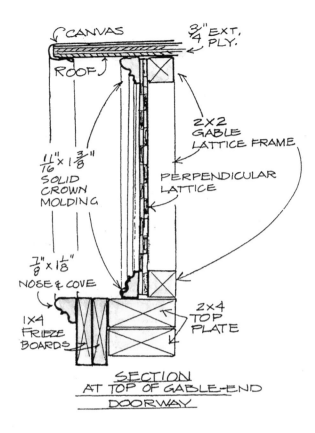

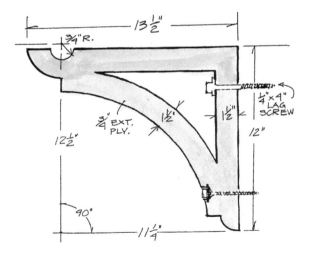

Brackets

To hold the roof poles, use a jigsaw to cut four brackets out of ¾" plywood, as shown in the plan. Screw them to the corner trim, using ¼"×4" lag screws. Secure the pole in the bracket with deck screws.

Paint

Finish the playhouse with the paint or stain of your choice.

Gambrel Roof Playhouse

This playful playhouse has extra room for a loft—add a foam mattress and a low railing, and your kids will have another whole dimension to their special place. The design is suitable for ages 3 to 8, and we've included plans for a kitchen so they can be independent and run their own house. The playhouse is designed for children, not adults, although in a pinch most adults can fit through the 2-foot door. The porch is the perfect gathering place for kids to sit around and discuss the topics of the day.

We used lightweight 2×4 lumber, sheathed in beveled cedar siding (clapboard) and roofed with asphalt shingles. The six easy-to-make windows are cut from ¾" exterior plywood using an electric jigsaw, and the top window can be flipped open and closed with a pulley set up inside the playhouse. The Dutch door allows for both ventilation and privacy; and if you (like one babysitter we know of) happen to get locked in by mischievous children, you can always escape through the upstairs window. . . .

MATERIALS

4		concrete blocks *for foundation*
3	12'	2×6 pressure-treated lumber *for base & porch*
4	8'	2×6 pressure-treated lumber *for base*
2	4'×8'	¾" A-C plywood *for floor*
2	12'	⁵⁄₄×6 pressure-treated lumber *for porch floor*
1	8'	⁵⁄₄×6 pressure-treated lumber *for porch floor*
2	10'	2×3 spruce *for wall frame*

Note: spruce, fir & pine should be treated with clear preservative for outdoor use

3	12'	2×3 spruce *for wall frame*
19	8'	2×3 spruce *for wall frame*
5	12'	2×6 construction fir *for rafters*
1	4'×4'	½" plywood *for gusset plates*
4	4'×8'	½" plywood *for roof*
1	12'	1×6 #2 construction fir *for ridge pole*

30 linear ft.		crown molding *for fascia boards*
3	16'	1×4 primed pine *for fascia boards*
100 sq. ft.		architectural asphalt shingles *for roof*
100 sq. ft.		roofing felt *for roof*
2lbs.		Roofing nails
64	6'	beveled cedar siding *for walls*
3	8'	2×2 clear cedar *for railings*
1	6'	⁵⁄₄×8 clear pine *for seat backs*
1	6'	1×10 clear pine *for seats*
1	8'	2×6 pressure-treated lumber *for window sills*
1	4'×8'	¾" A-C plywood *for windows*
5	8'	1×6 tongue & groove clear cedar *for door*
4		hinges
2		handles

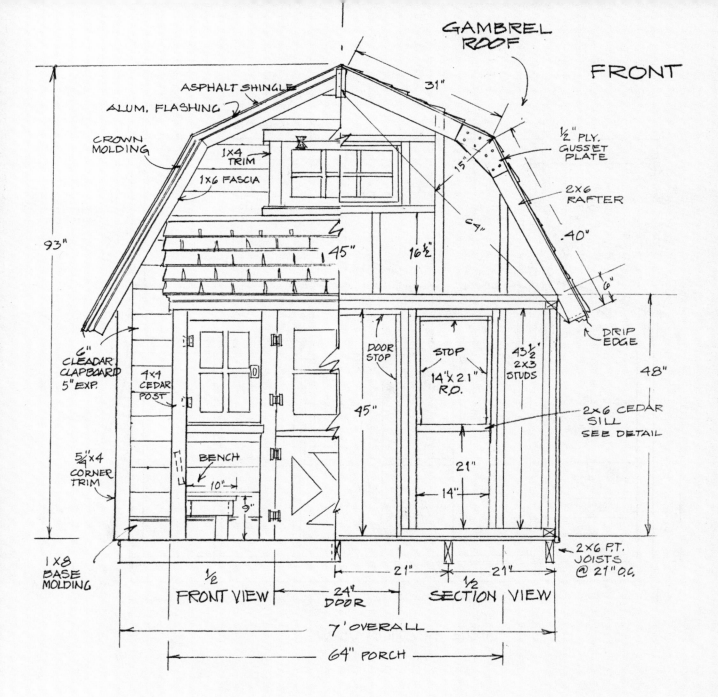

GAMBREL ROOF

FRONT

ASPHALT SHINGLE

ALUM. FLASHING

CROWN MOLDING

1×4 TRIM

1×6 FASCIA

31"

½" PLY. GUSSET PLATE

2×6 RAFTER

15"

16½"

.40"

6"

45"

6"

DRIP EDGE

48"

93"

6" CLEADAR CLAPBOARD 5" EXP.

4×4 CEDAR POST

DOOR STOP

STOP

14"×21" R.O.

43½" 2×3 STUDS

45"

2×6 CEDAR SILL SEE DETAIL

BENCH

10"

9"

21"

14"

5¾"×4 CORNER TRIM

1×8 BASE MOLDING

2×6 P.T. JOISTS @ 21" O.C.

½ FRONT VIEW

24" DOOR

21"

½ SECTION VIEW

21"

7' OVERALL

64" PORCH

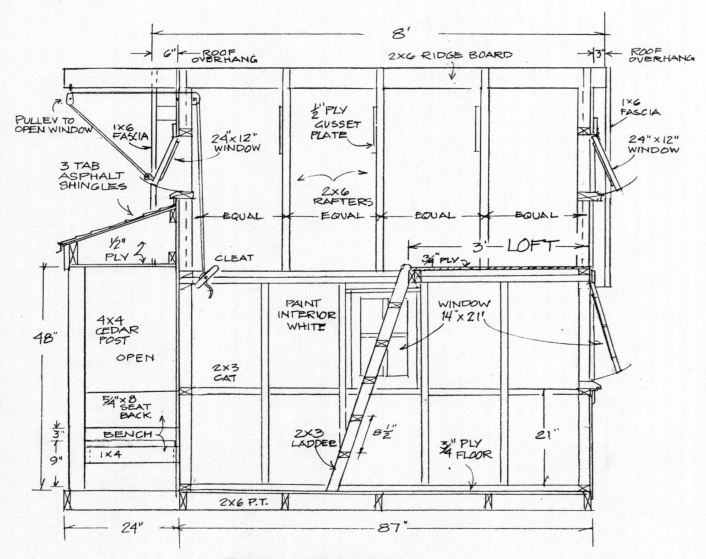

SIDE SECTION VIEW

8'

6" ROOF OVERHANG

2×6 RIDGE BOARD

3" ROOF OVERHANG

PULLEV TO OPEN WINDOW

1×6 FASCIA

24"×12" WINDOW

½" PLY GUSSET PLATE

1×6 FASCIA

24"×12" WINDOW

3 TAB ASPHALT SHINGLES

2×6 RAFTERS

½" PLY

EQUAL   EQUAL   EQUAL   EQUAL

3' LOFT

CLEAT

¾" PLY

4×4 CEDAR POST

OPEN

PAINT INTERIOR WHITE

WINDOW 14"×21"

48"

2×3 CAT

5/4"×8 SEAT BACK.

2×3 LADDER

8½"

21"

BENCH

1×4

3"

¾" PLY FLOOR

9"

2×6 P.T.

24"   87"

Windows

We really like the open, airy feel to this playhouse; this is largely because we put in so many windows. Not to worry—these windows are inexpensive and easy to make. For maximum light, there are five 14"×21" and two 24"×12" (loft) windows, all made the same way.

Build the window openings to the above dimensions, making sure the corners are square. (The diagonals should be equal.)

From ¾" exterior plywood, cut pieces to fit the window openings. They may have to be tapered slightly on the opening side, in order to close freely. Cut out the window (lite) openings using an electric jig saw.

From a piece of ⅛" Plexiglas, cut pieces 1" taller and wider than the window openings, and screw them to the inside of the windows. Tip: Since Plexiglas expands and contracts during temperature changes, drill oversized pilot holes for the screws, and fill with clear silicone sealant before installing the screws.

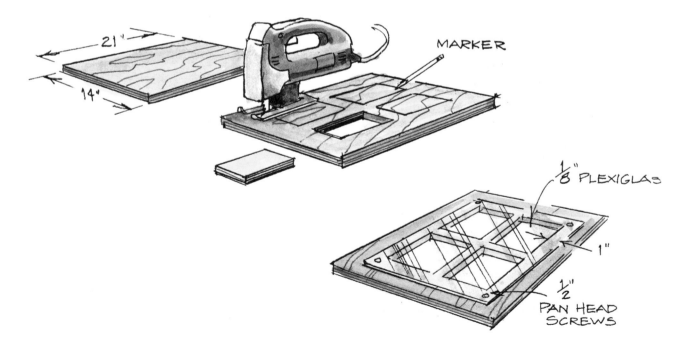

Cut a piece of 2¼"-wide window trim ⅛" taller than the window (for clearance), attach two "H" type hinges to trim and window, and nail the trim (and attached window) to the wall frame.

Nail the other pieces of trim to the wall frame; cut and nail strips of 1×2 to the inside, to stop the window from swinging in.

Add a wooden knob to the outside, and a hook & eye fastener to the inside.

Since kids love to operate things, rig a rope & pulley from the end of the ridge beam to the bottom of the loft window (see Side Section View).

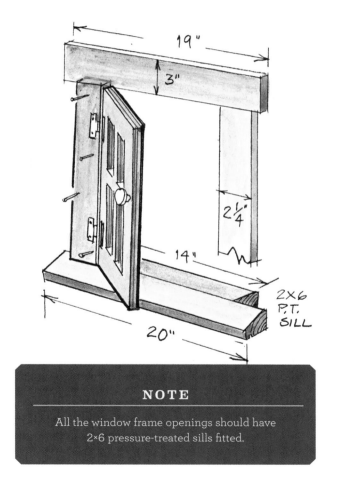

19"

3"

2¼"

14"

20"

2×6 P.T. SILL

NOTE

All the window frame openings should have 2×6 pressure-treated sills fitted.

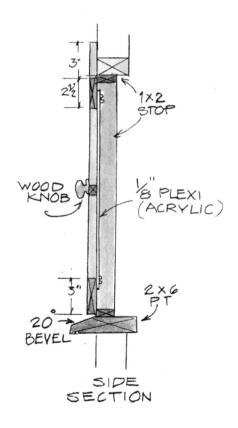

3"

2½"

1×2 STOP

WOOD KNOB

⅛" PLEXI (ACRYLIC)

3"

2×6 P.T

20 BEVEL

SIDE SECTION

WINDOW

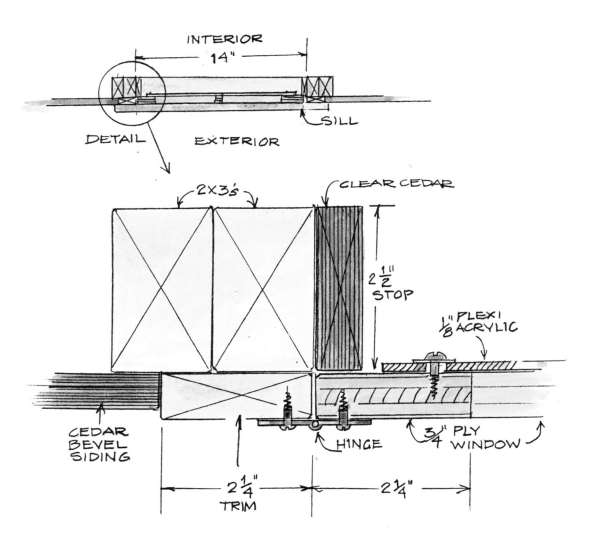

INTERIOR
14"

SILL

DETAIL   EXTERIOR

2X3's

CLEAR CEDAR

2½"
STOP

⅛" PLEXI
ACRYLIC

CEDAR
BEVEL
SIDING

HINGE

¾" PLY
WINDOW

2¼"
TRIM

2¼"

213

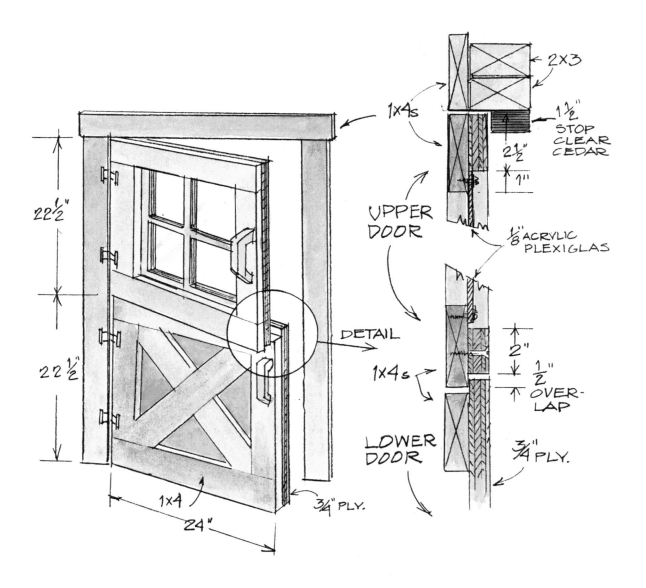

2X3

1x4s

UPPER
DOOR

1½"
STOP
CLEAR
CEDAR

2½"

1"

⅛"ACRYLIC
PLEXIGLAS

DETAIL

1x4s

2"

½"
OVER-
LAP

LOWER
DOOR

¾" PLY.

22½"

22½"

1x4

24"

¾" PLY.

Door

We built a child-sized Dutch door that allows kids to have ventilation while still maintaining a sense of privacy. Frame the door first and construct the two door sections separately, with the top section overlapping the bottom. The X-shaped brace reinforces the bottom half and the window is easily made out of Plexiglas.

NOTE

An optional play kitchen can be built separately from the playhouse and installed later. For the sink, use an ordinary plastic tub recessed into the countertop; the faucet can be wooden dowels of various thicknesses.

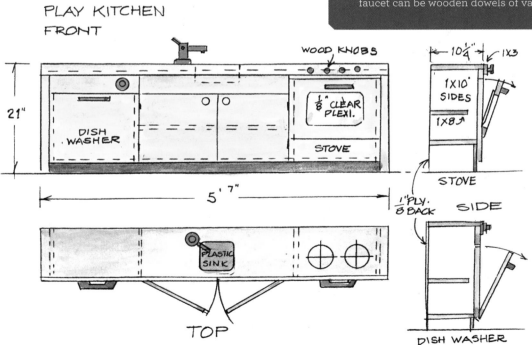

PLAY KITCHEN FRONT

WOOD KNOBS

21"

DISH WASHER

⅛" CLEAR PLEXI.

STOVE

5' 7"

10¼"   1X3

1X10 SIDES

1X8

STOVE

⅛" PLY. BACK

SIDE

PLASTIC SINK

TOP

DISH WASHER

215

Even a tiny Brooklyn backyard
can have a playhouse getaway.

4

More Advanced Projects

This section is more about inspiration than instruction—we give you some examples of applied building techniques rather than detailed plans and materials. All three structures are very different from each other and slightly more ambitious than some of the previous ones. For those of you who prefer designing your own projects, elements can be taken from here to help you develop your own unique designs.

Artist's Studio

Many people find it beneficial to have a defined workspace close to, but separate from, the house. This studio was built in Cornwall, UK by artist Toby Haynes; he needed light, space, and specific areas for drawing and watercolor work, oil painting, and writing.

Your requirements will most likely be different. Take into consideration the need for plumbing and electricity and how much natural light you want to allow in; and also whether the building is for year-round use or just for the summer. Make sure there is adequate ceiling height for easels and other studio equipment. For a photographer's studio, you will need to allow for backdrops, studio lights and storage.

As you'll see on pages 228 and 229, much of the furniture in the studio was made from remaining scrap wood from the project.

Because the posts supporting the walls, floor and roof are sunk into the ground, this building needs no foundations or leveling of the area—making it ideal for an uneven or sloping site. Although easier to build than the timber-frame on page 230, it is very sturdy, and the exposed timbers give the interior a traditional feel. This studio is 20'×13', but the dimensions can be altered to suit. The walls are made in small sections, so it is (just barely) a manageable project for one person. In the rainy southwest of England, pressure-treated wood was used throughout; but in any case, the posts should be certified for ground contact. As a bonus, most of the fittings and furniture are made out of wood left over from construction.

The 6×6 posts need to be dug in deeply enough to resist frost heave; in this case, 12' posts proved long enough to allow for 7'-6" walls and a generous air-space between floor and damp ground. Set out and dig all the post holes; prop all the posts in place with temporary braces, as you check and adjust the alignment and measure the diagonals. Nail a temporary rail along the outside face of each wall at the top, using a level to establish a consistent height for the posts. Concrete the posts securely, and trim the tops carefully with a sharp timber saw.

Fix the 2×10 bottom plates using two ½"×6" lag screws per joint, and the joists with deck screws or joist hangers. For a floor this wide, run a 2×10 girder the length of the building under the center of the joists; this can be simply screwed to the center posts

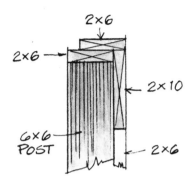

TOP PLATES

2×6

2×6

2×10

6×6
POST

2×6

CORNER DETAIL

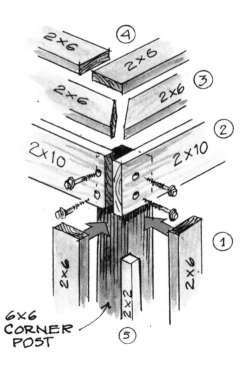

2×6 ④
2×6

2×6 ③
2×6

2×10 ② 2×10

① ①

2×6 2×6

6×6
CORNER
POST

2×2

⑤

of the two short sides.

Fit the 2×10 top wall plates in place of the temporary rails, making them extend 1½" above the tops of the posts. Fit a vertical 2×6 to the outside of each post to bring its face flush with the top and bottom plates. Lay the floorboards now—this will make it easier to move around, use stepladders, etc.

Cut 2×6s to rest flat on top of the posts and against the inside of the 2×10 top plates; miter the corners where they meet. Screw them to posts and plates. Add a second, overlapping course of 2×6s, flush with the outside of the wall plate. This increases the strength greatly.

Cut a 2×6 to fit horizontally between two of the posts. This is the base plate for that section of the wall. Make 2×6 studwork to fit, and if you are using ready-made windows (as here), allow ¼" for adjustments on all sides of the window. Notch the top outside of the studs so that, when swung up into place, they will finish flush with the outside of the posts and wall plates. Screw the wall section to the floor, posts, and top plate, and continue around the rest of the walls in the same way.

Mark the center of one gable end, on both top and bottom plates, and nail a temporary rail so that one side aligns with the two marks. Check that it's vertical. You can then clamp one of your rafter timbers to this "mast," resting the other end on the wall plate, and try different angles. Once you're happy with it, simply draw a line down where the mast and

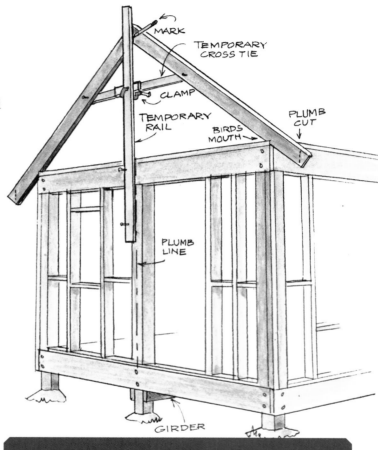

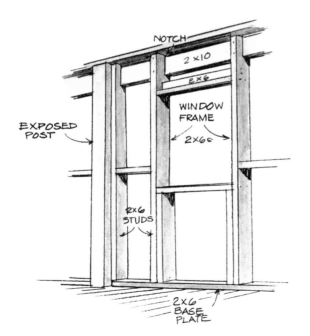

rafter meet at the center: this will be your vertical mark for the ridge and bird's-mouth cuts. The bird's mouth will start exactly where the rafter now rests on the outside of the top plate; copy the angle from the ridge using a sliding bevel. Be aware that, once the bird's mouth is cut, the whole roof will sit 1½" lower. Mark and cut notches for the purlins. The roof covering here is corrugated sheets, so the 2×3 purlins were spaced accordingly. Mark your first rafter to use as the pattern for all the others. Make plywood gusset plates to strengthen the joint, and cut the notch for the ridge board. Fit cross-ties to the roof trusses; in the loft area, these will be removed later. The tempo-

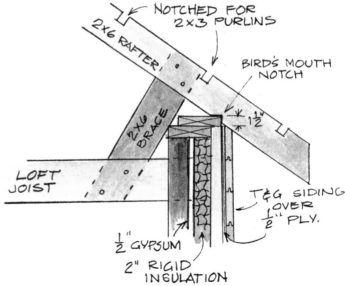

NOTCHED FOR 2×3 PURLINS

2×6 RAFTER

BIRD'S MOUTH NOTCH

1½"

2×6 BRACE

LOFT JOIST

T&G SIDING OVER ½" PLY.

½" GYPSUM

2" RIGID INSULATION

rary mast makes it relatively easy to place the first roof truss while you fasten the rafter tails with screws or metal plates; do the same at the other end of the roof, and nail a temporary purlin to both ends while you lift the remaining trusses into position. The central roof truss is stronger and more elaborate, for appearance and to support the staircase. Screw on the ridge board and purlins to complete the roof frame. Note the use of temporary diagonal braces during this process—indispensable if you're working alone.

Attach the loft floor joists with screws through the top plates; brace them to the rafters for mutual support, before removing the cross-ties.

Cover the building, apart from windows and doorway, with ½" exterior plywood, followed by tarpaper. (The original has Tyvek housewrap, but this is frustratingly slippery stuff!) Fit the windows, shimming as necessary before nailing into place and

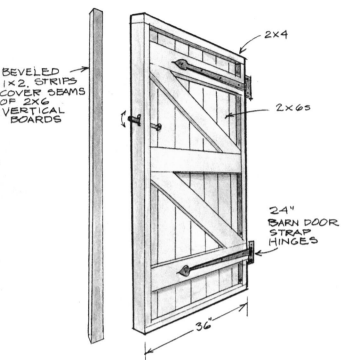

BEVELED 1×2 STRIPS COVER SEAMS OF 2×6 VERTICAL BOARDS

2×4

2×6s

24" BARN DOOR STRAP HINGES

36"

sealing with foam sealant. (Be careful: it's called "expanding foam" for a reason . . .) For an old-world feel, make the door of 2×6s "ledged & braced" (fitted with horizontal and diagonal struts), framed by 2×4s on edge, and cover the joins in the boards with beveled 1×2s (the result will be heavy) and to complete the effect, a hand-forged Suffolk latch and immense barn-door hinges that creak atmospherically.

Tongue & groove horizontal sheathing is a good choice for practicality and weather-resistance, especially with three coats of acrylic exterior varnish;

alternatively, you could paint it or let it weather naturally. The simple entrance steps are made of 3×12s to enhance the impression of solidity.

Inside, the staircase is designed to take up minimum space, and is suspended from the central roof truss. The walls are covered with 2" polystyrene insulation bonded to the plywood, with foil-backed plasterboard on top. An electrician was hired for the extensive wiring before the plasterboard went up. A narrow wooden ceiling, fitted with recessed lights, conceals the plywood gusset plates in the roof.

Much of the studio furniture comes from the leftovers. Pressure-treated wood takes sanding and routing surprisingly well, though it's not easy to plane by hand. You can make useful and distinctive items out of even the shabbiest pieces.

The Timber-Frame

Traditional timber framing looks great, and is very strong and durable. Although it takes time to make a mortise and tenon joint and secure it with a wooden peg (treenail), the sense of pride and accomplishment is well worth the effort. This is the way buildings were made for centuries, by carpenters using simple hand tools—mainly a saw, mallet and sharp chisel.

Many people, even professionals, confuse timber-framing with post & beam construction. Both methods use heavy timbers, which accounts for the confusion that exists between the two. Traditional timber-framing uses difficult-to-make mortise & tenon joints secured with wooden pegs (tree nails), whereas post & beam often uses simple lap joints and even metal fasteners to hold the pieces together. Various materials have been used to fill between the timbers, such as wattle and daub (sticks and mud), bricks, stucco and straw. Timber-frame structures can be finished off in numerous ways, just like a modern stick-built house—among them, plywood, clapboard, board & batten, shingles, or even stucco. Today, houses are generally stick built with 2×4s or 2×6s, and sheathed with plywood to stiffen the frame and keep it from racking.

HERE ARE A FEW TIPS TO MAKE THE JOB EASIER

- Use pressure-treated wood for the sill plates and floor joists, Northern pine for the rest.

- Invest in a coarse-cut saw (we used the Bahco Profcut and Superior saws) to cut the big lumber and lap joints. A circular saw and a chisel can also be used for lap joints, but may be harder to control accurately. A framer's slick is useful for finishing (paring) tenons and lap joints.

- Use a marking gauge to find the center of timbers, mark tenons and mortises, etc. For repetitive joints, make a cardboard template, and use a tenon-sized piece of wood to test each mortise for fit.

- With an electric drill and ¾" auger bit, bore out most of the waste material from the mortises, and finish with a 1½" framing chisel. Mark around the mortise with shallow chisel cuts before drilling, to prevent splitting out the edges.

- When the sill lap joints are finished, cut temporary pegs to hold them in place while you adjust the timbers. Use a long level and a framing square to set them in place, on blocks if necessary. Make sure the diagonals are equal.

- Temporarily set the top plates upside-down on the leveled sills while you make and fit the corner posts, braces and studs. That way you won't have to keep lifting the heavy top plates every time you want to check a joint for fit (but you will have to remember which side is which when it's upside-down . . .).

- Number each joint with a chisel or permanent marker as you work. And never assume it fits— check it before you try to assemble the whole frame. Each new joint tightens the whole structure and leaves less margin for error.

- This building is designed to have vertical sheathing boards nailed to the outside of the frame. If you intend to use horizontal shiplap, tongue & groove or clapboard, supplement the main posts with 2×4 studs, set 24" apart; this will allow you to insulate between the studs and cover them with drywall.

- Draw plans on ¼" grid paper; for a 10'×12' building, use two squares to the foot, or for a larger building, one square to the foot. If you're planning something really big, consult an architect or structural engineer with experience of timber-framing. For ease of access, consider placing the door at the highest point of the site.

- Most lumber yards and home-improvement centers don't stock material suitable for timber-framing, but they should be able to order it for you; if you live in the country or have access to a saw mill, you may be able to get the wood significantly cheaper. Northern pine will be a lot lighter than oak, in case you don't have an army of helpers.

- If you do have helpers, why not have a timber-framing party?

How to Build a Timber-Frame

Lay out the shed with mason's string and four wooden stakes. Use a level and check the diagonals for square.

Cut lap joints on the ends of the 6×6 pressure-treated sill beams, using a coarse-cut timber saw. Set out the base, level and square, on concrete blocks.

With a framing chisel, cut 2"×2" mortises through the lap joints (remembering that the corner posts are 5"×5"). Place a piece of wood under the mortise to avoid splitting out, and turn the beam over to finish the cut from the other side. Use a carpenter's square to make sure the sides of the mortise are straight.

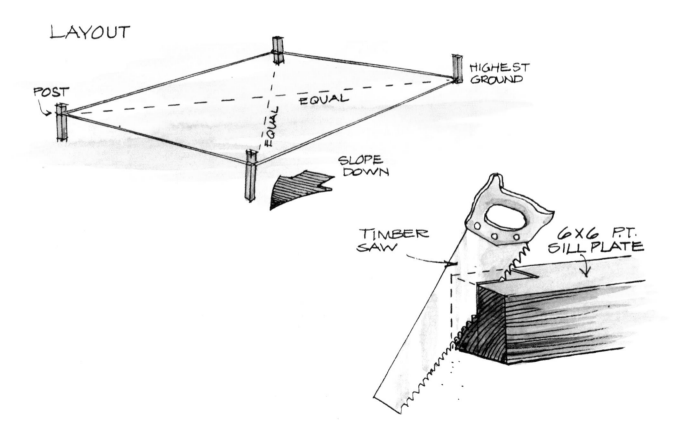

LAYOUT

POST

HIGHEST GROUND

EQUAL

EQUAL

SLOPE DOWN

TIMBER SAW

6×6 P.T. SILL PLATE

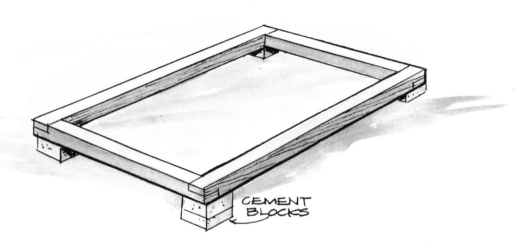

CEMENT
BLOCKS

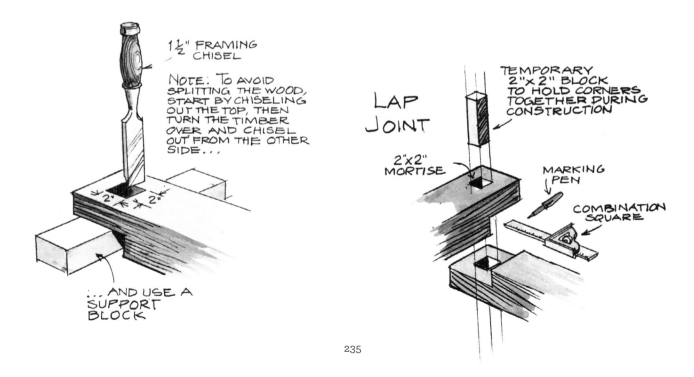

1½" FRAMING
CHISEL

NOTE: TO AVOID
SPLITTING THE WOOD,
START BY CHISELING
OUT THE TOP, THEN
TURN THE TIMBER
OVER AND CHISEL
OUT FROM THE OTHER
SIDE...

2"   2"

... AND USE A
SUPPORT
BLOCK

LAP
JOINT

2"x2"
MORTISE

TEMPORARY
2"x 2" BLOCK
TO HOLD CORNERS
TOGETHER DURING
CONSTRUCTION

MARKING
PEN

COMBINATION
SQUARE

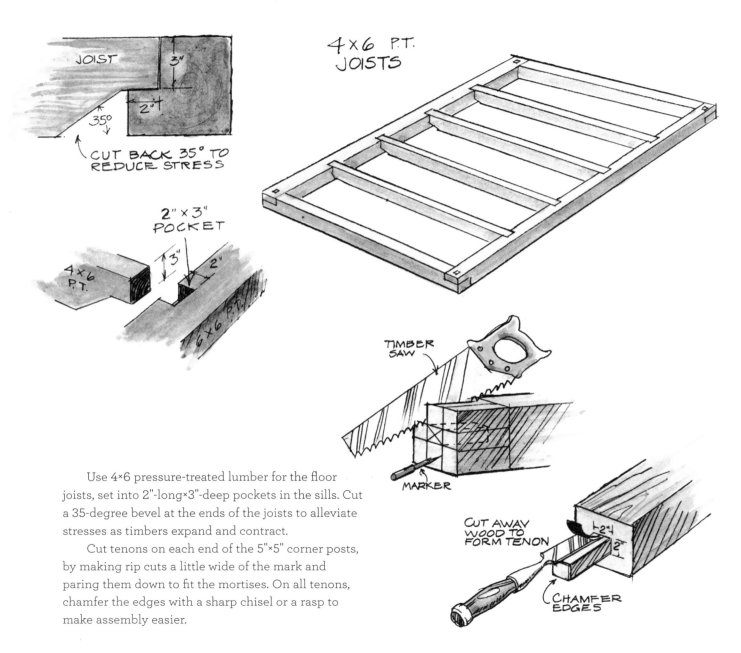

JOIST

3"

2"

35°

CUT BACK 35° TO
REDUCE STRESS

4×6 P.T.
JOISTS

2" × 3"
POCKET

3"

2"

4×6
P.T.

6×6 P.T.

TIMBER
SAW

MARKER

CUT AWAY
WOOD TO
FORM TENON

2"

2"

CHAMFER
EDGES

Use 4×6 pressure-treated lumber for the floor
joists, set into 2"-long×3"-deep pockets in the sills. Cut
a 35-degree bevel at the ends of the joists to alleviate
stresses as timbers expand and contract.

Cut tenons on each end of the 5"×5" corner posts,
by making rip cuts a little wide of the mark and
paring them down to fit the mortises. On all tenons,
chamfer the edges with a sharp chisel or a rasp to
make assembly easier.

STUDS & BRACES

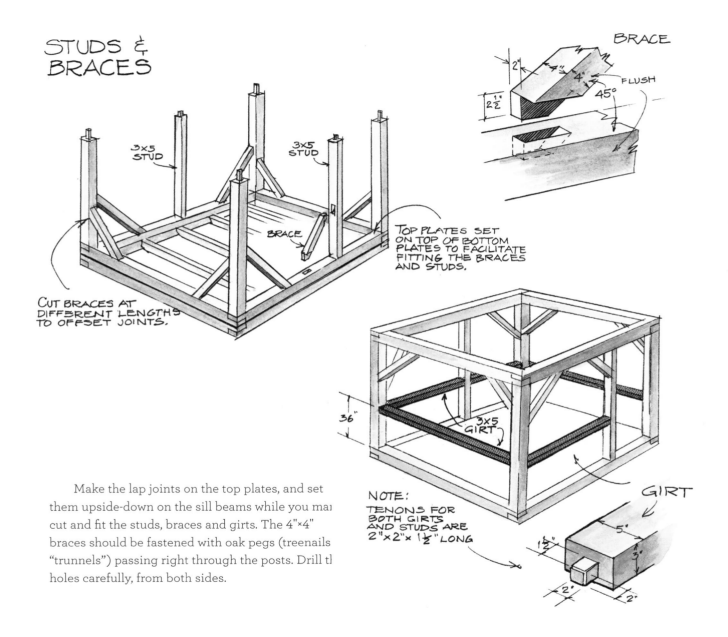

3x5 STUD

3x5 STUD

BRACE

Cut braces at different lengths to offset joints.

Top plates set on top of bottom plates to facilitate fitting the braces and studs.

BRACE

2"

4"

2½"

FLUSH

45°

36"

3x5 GIRT

NOTE: TENONS FOR BOTH GIRTS AND STUDS ARE 2"x2"x 1½" LONG

GIRT

5"

3"

1½"

2"

2"

Make the lap joints on the top plates, and set them upside-down on the sill beams while you ma[r] cut and fit the studs, braces and girts. The 4"×4" braces should be fastened with oak pegs (treenails "trunnels") passing right through the posts. Drill t[l] holes carefully, from both sides.

Cut lap joints in the tops of the 3"×5" rafters, and cut bird's-mouth notches where they will rest on the top plates. Mark the exact location by laying trial pieces on the floor. Use the first rafter as a pattern for all the rest. Cut the rafter tails long enough to deflect rainwater, but make sure there is enough clearance for the door (if it is to open outwards). Use treenails at the lap joints and at the top plates.

Once everything fits, mark and cut corresponding mortises in the sill plates for the 3"×5" studs, then gather your army of helpers to raise the building. It can be tricky to fit the girts and braces at the same time—you may find it easier to assemble an end wall (or "bent") on the base first, lift it into place and repeat the procedure at the other end, before fitting the other two walls and locking them all together with the final top plates. Nail the bents to the sills with temporary diagonal braces until the walls are finished. Assemble the rafters, and nail a temporary ridge board to the peaks until you are ready to enclose the building.

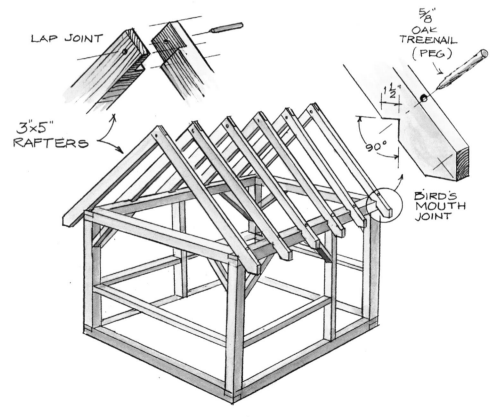

LAP JOINT

3"×5" RAFTERS

⅝" OAK TREENAIL (PEG)

1½"

90°

BIRD'S MOUTH JOINT

Teahouse

Call it what you will: it's a teahouse, pool pavilion, tiki hut—even a garden folly. It's really a place to sit down, relax, and enjoy the garden or an afternoon's lounging on a plush divan with a good book (such as this one). It's also ideal for entertaining guests on a summer evening; and if you have a beautiful view across a mountain range with a serene sunset in the background, that would work too...

We've chosen to give the builder detailed instructions on specific elements of design and construction. The size and details can be varied infinitely. The materials list will depend upon your needs. You might construct a slate floor at ground level or raise the base higher and have steps leading up to it. The roof could be covered with thatch, cedar or asphalt shingles, or even copper or tile depending on what part of the country you live in and the style of your house.

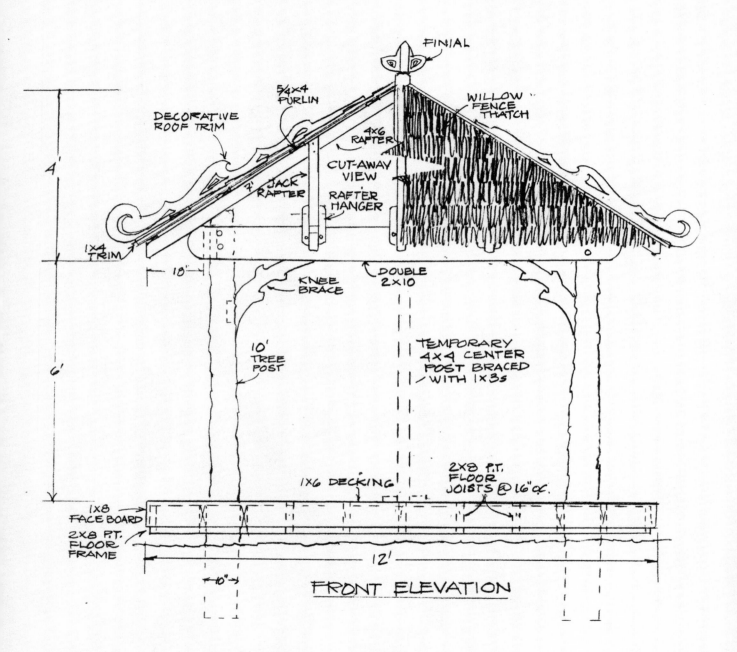

FINIAL

DECORATIVE
ROOF TRIM

5/4×4
PURLIN

4×6
RAFTER

WILLOW
FENCE
THATCH

CUT-AWAY
VIEW

JACK
RAFTER

RAFTER
HANGER

1×4
TRIM

18"

KNEE
BRACE

DOUBLE
2×10

10'
TREE
POST

TEMPORARY
4×4 CENTER
POST BRACED
WITH 1×3s

1×6 DECKING

2×8 P.T.
FLOOR
JOISTS @ 16" O.C.

1×8
FACE BOARD

2×8 P.T.
FLOOR
FRAME

12'

10"

FRONT ELEVATION

4'

6'

Corner Posts

Start with four cedar, locust, or juniper trees with straight trunks approximately 12' high and 9"–10" in diameter at the butt end. Make sure they are free of bugs and rot. If you don't have access to suitable trees, you should be able to find ready-cut posts at your local nursery or lumberyard.

Saw off the branches, being careful not to scar the main trunk. Use a chisel and mallet to cut away any surface protrusions that might cause injury, and sand using a grinder with smooth grit.

SHARP BRANCHLET

BRANCH NUB SANDED SMOOTH

NOTE

Some types of trees, such as juniper, red cedar, and hickory, look great if you leave branch nubs sticking out slightly, but these should still be rounded off. Finish the posts with two coats of clear preservative.

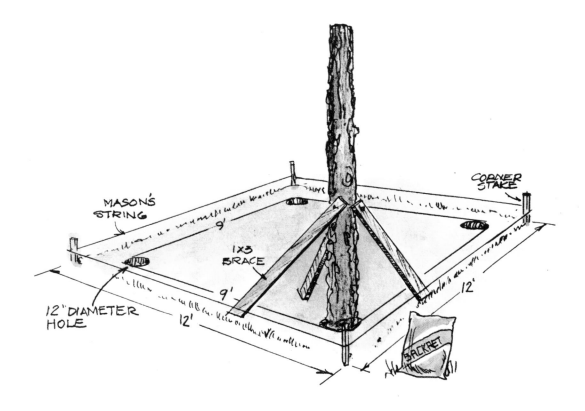

MASON'S STRING

CORNER STAKE

1×3 BRACE

12" DIAMETER HOLE

9'

9'

12'

12'

BACKFILL

Setting the Posts

Make sure your furniture will fit the floor space, by plotting it onto grid paper or simply arranging it on site. Set out the perimeter of the floor using mason's string and stakes, and a second square 18" inside this line all round. (A 12' square will therefore contain a 9' square.) Dig four post holes, deep enough to go below the frost line, at the marked corners of the inner square. The posts don't need to be exactly equal heights—you can trim them later. Set each post so that the outside corner is plumb (vertical) using a long level. Check that the posts are square with each other by measuring the diagonals between two opposite corners. The distances should be equal—but since trees don't come in uniform sizes or perfectly straight, you may have to experiment to get the best alignment: it matters most at the top and bottom, where an accurate square will make framing the roof and floor much easier. Use 1×3 boards to brace and hold each post in place while you backfill with concrete mix (usually a bag per hole), and allow the concrete to cure overnight.

The Deck

Cut a pressure-treated 4×6 girder to the length of the floor, and bolt it across the two front posts, extending 18" beyond each, at ground level. Make sure it's level, or your floor won't be! Do the same across the rear posts, checking that both girders are at exactly the same height. Rest 2×8 pressure-treated rim joists across the ends of the girders (from front to back of the floor) and extending equally beyond each, toenail in place and join into a square with two more 2×8s, using three 3" coated star drive screws per corner. Use metal joist hangers to attach 2×8 pressure-treated joists at 16" centers across the girders; toenail the joists to the girders. If the span is more than 10', lay a central 4×6 pressure-treated girder under the floor to support the joists. (If you are working on a slope, the girders may have to rest on short posts of their own to eliminate the bounce . . .) Box the posts in with pieces of 2×8, to support the ends of the deck boards.

Attach the decking to the floor joists using 2" coated star drive screws, countersunk below the surface of the deck; use a pencil or suitable piece of scrap wood to maintain an equal gap between deck boards. Take time to fit the decking carefully around the irregular posts—a certain amount of trial and error is involved.

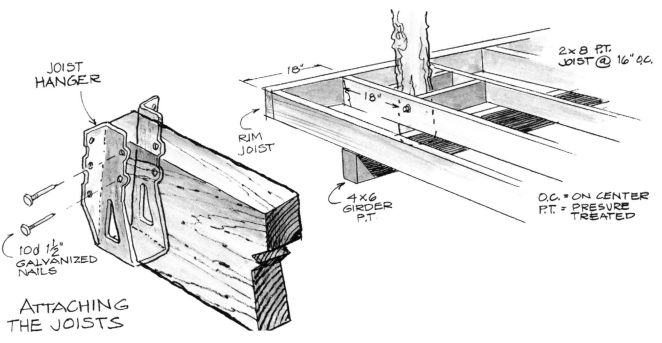

JOIST HANGER

18"

18"

RIM JOIST

2×8 P.T. JOIST @ 16" O.C.

4×6 GIRDER P.T.

O.C. = ON CENTER
P.T. = PRESSURE TREATED

10d 1½" GALVANIZED NAILS

ATTACHING THE JOISTS

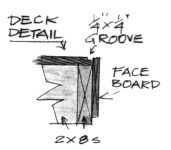

DECK DETAIL

¼"×¼" GROOVE

FACE BOARD

2×8 s

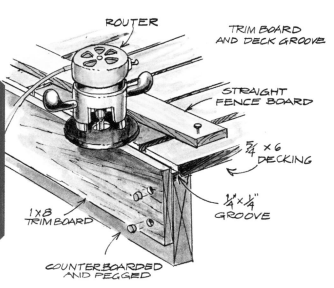

ROUTER

TRIM BOARD AND DECK GROOVE

STRAIGHT FENCE BOARD

5/4 × 6 DECKING

¼"×¼" GROOVE

1×8 TRIM BOARD

COUNTERBOARDED AND PEGGED

BUILDING TIP

For a sleeker look, select clear 1×8 boards to trim the edge of the deck. Screw them to the outside of the pressure-treated rim joists, but raised flush with the deck boards and mitered at the corners. Counterbore the screw holes first, and hide the screw heads with pegs made of the same type of wood, sanded flush.

Roof Framing

Measure at least 6' up from the deck, and attach 2×8 pressure-treated wall plates around the tops of the posts, using ½"×4" lag screws. For extra strength, add a cap plate horizontally to the top of the wall plates and posts.

Find the center point of the deck and erect a 10'-6"-high 4×4 post, held in place with temporary 1×3 cross-braces attached to the wall plates, and blocks or wedges at the base. Notch the corners of

the wall plates to receive the corner rafters. Cut four 4×6 pressure-treated corner rafters; screw them to the center post and corner posts. Cut and install 4×6 pressure-treated jack rafters as shown (see Roof Framing Plan). Cut off and remove the lower section of the center post. Screw 5/4" pressure-treated purlins across the rafters every 2', and cover the roof with ¾" pressure-treated plywood.

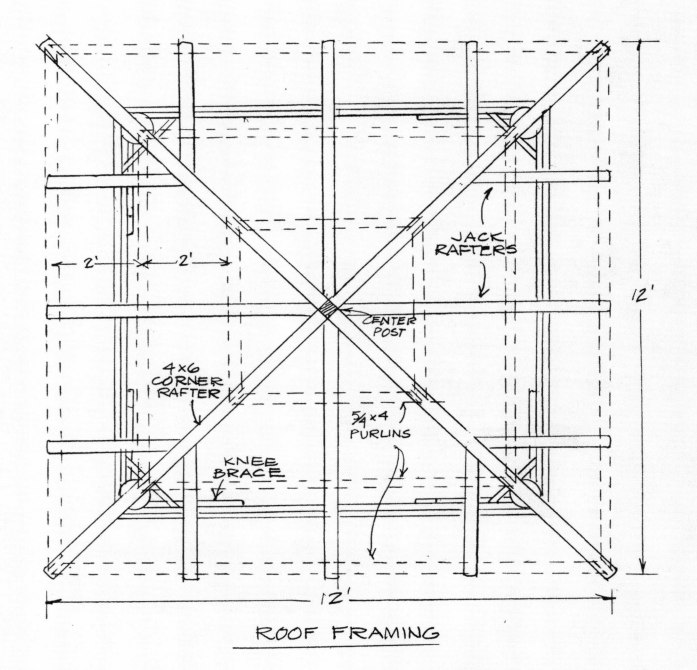

JACK
RAFTERS

CENTER
POST

4×6
CORNER
RAFTER

5/4×4
PURLINS

KNEE
BRACE

2' 2'

12'

12'

ROOF FRAMING

Roofing

Cover the roof with #30 roofing felt, and nail 18"-high rolls of willow reed fencing, using 1" wide-headed nails or fencing staples and overlapping each row by 6". Leave a 1½" gap where the thatching meets the corner rafters, to allow for the decorative trim. Cover the ends of the thatch with 1×4s and caulk any gaps.

Decorative Roof Trim

A garden retreat such as this cries out for a distinctive motif to avoid being just an ordinary, functional structure. The trim shown here, cut from a 7'-long pressure-treated 2×10, gives the building an exotic air. Cut the profile with an electric jigsaw.

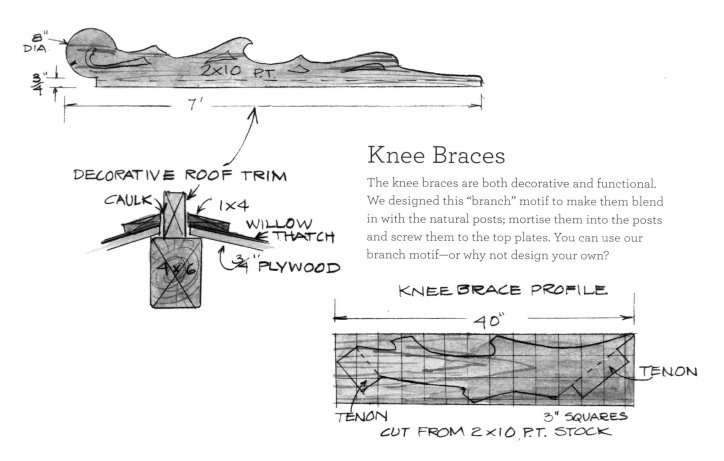

Knee Braces

The knee braces are both decorative and functional. We designed this "branch" motif to make them blend in with the natural posts; mortise them into the posts and screw them to the top plates. You can use our branch motif—or why not design your own?

Rafter Hangers

Cut the rafter hangers from 2×10s and screw them to the top plates and the jack rafters. The rafter hangers function as "hurricane hangers," securing the roof firmly when heavy winds blow (see Plan—Front Elevation).

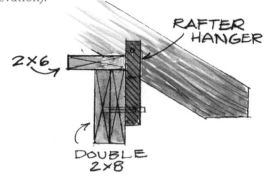

Stain

To further protect the pressure-treated wood and for a warmer look, we stained it with Minwax cherry stain for a rich, teak-like color.

The Finial

Cut the finial from a 2×6 and notch the two pieces together. Attach it to the center post, using a hanger screw. The finial represents the lotus flower, the symbol of divine cosmic harmony.

Afterword

A recent trip to the beautiful English countryside has given us many ideas for future backyard and garden designs. We saw some of the famous gardens maintained by such organizations as The National Trust and English Heritage; but we also shamelessly peered over the hedges of small cottage gardens in our quest for the unusual. Of course, we are always on the lookout for interesting buildings, whether at home or abroad; and here are just a few of the many unique structures we have encountered on our travels. You can replicate them or use them as a springboard for your own creativity.

Enjoy your backyard building.

ACKNOWLEDGMENTS

We would like to thank our editor, Ann Treistman,
for her vision, enthusiasm and commitment;
copy-editor Toby Haynes, for his clarity and attention
to detail; photographer Simon Jutras, for the beautiful
cover photograph; and book designer Nick Caruso,
for combining all the elements.

Antique hardware—hinges, knobs, latches.
Van Dyke's Restorers
www.vandykes.com

Cabinet hardware—slides, hinges, knobs, pulls
Woodworker's Supply
www.woodworker.com

Hand tools—cable cutters, wrenches
Harbor Freight Tools
www.harborfreight.com

Lumber, hardware, tools & paint
www.lowes.com

Power tools—cordless drills, miter saws
Hitachi Koki Co., Ltd.
www.hitachi-koki.com

Wood stains
Minwax
www.minwax.com

Rope—synthetic Hempex rope for railings

R&W Rope Warehouse
www.rwrope.com

Glue for exterior fabrications
Titebond III
www.titebond.com

Epoxy for extra strong waterproof bonding
www.westsystem.com

Construction adhesive—PL400 urethane
www.loctiteproducts.com

Barn sash windows made from recycled milk bottles
www.recycledproductsco.com

Marine supplies—stainless steel wire cable, shackles, blocks, pulleys
Defender Marine & Boat Supplies
www.defender.com